AF566798

AMERICA
IN THE
ASIAN CENTURY

OBSERVER RESEARCH FOUNDATION

Building Partnerships for a Global India

Observer Research Foundation (ORF) is a not-for-profit, multidisciplinary public policy think tank engaged in developing and discussing policy alternatives on a wide-range of issues of national and international significance. Some of ORF's key areas of research include international relations, security affairs, politics and governance, resources management and economy and development. The fundamental objective of ORF is to influence formulation of policies for building a strong and prosperous India in a globalised world.

ORF pursues these goals by providing informed and productive inputs, in-depth research and stimulating discussions. Set up in the early 1990s during the troubled period of India's transition from a protected economy to its new engagement with the international economic order, ORF examines critical policy problems facing the country and helps develop coherent policy responses in a rapidly changing global environment.

As an independent think tank, ORF develops and publishes informed and viable inputs for policymakers in the Government and for the political and business leadership of the country. It maintains a range of informal contacts with politicians, policymakers, civil servants, business leaders and the media, in India, and abroad. ORF publications are distributed widely to government officials and legislators, business leaders, journalists, and academics.

ORF's principal research divisions are: the ORF Centre for International Relations, the ORF Institute of Security Studies, the ORF Centre for Economy and Development, the ORF Centre for Resources Management, and the ORF Centre for Politics and Governance. Headquartered in New Delhi, ORF has chapters in Chennai, Mumbai and an upcoming centre in Kolkatta.

More information about the Foundation is available at its website www.orfonline.org

AMERICA IN THE ASIAN CENTURY

EDITED AND INTRODUCED BY

MAHARAJAKRISHNA RASGOTRA

This edition first published 2013

AMARYLLIS

An imprint of Manjul Publishing House Pvt. Ltd.
7/32, Ansari Road, Daryaganj,
New Delhi 110 002
Email: amaryllis@amaryllis.co.in
Website: www.amaryllis.co.in

Registered Office:
10, Nishat Colony, Bhopal 462 003, M.P., India

ISBN: 978-93-81506-28-8

Printed and Bound in India by
Thomson Press (India) Limited

Contents

Introduction

This book, authored jointly by scholars working with me in the Observer Research Foundation (ORF), tells the story of the USA's extensive and vigorous engagement in all regions of Asia, from Japan in the continent's Northeast, through Southeast and South Asia, the Persian Gulf, the Arab region and Central Asia to Russia in the West. The idea of writing this book arose during an in-house discussion at ORF about the speculation – much of it originating in the US itself – about America's decline and the advent of an Asian Century dominated by China. Because of assertive claims by China of its core interests and rights in land and seas on its periphery, the questions on people's mind these days are: Will China rule the world? Or will the USA, the prevailing pre-eminent power, also have a role in ensuring balance, peace, security and stability in Asia in the twenty-first century?

India's future role was also considered and it was felt that because of its size and power potential, India's role is bound to be of considerable importance, but the contest for dominance in Asia in the foreseeable future will primarily be between China and the United States. Set out in the following paragraphs is the course our discussion took on the roles of these two Great Powers in the twenty-first century.

China's claim to be the eponym of the century is clear enough: it is the largest country in Asia with a formidable army, a strong air force, an expanding navy, and a huge arsenal of nuclear armed missiles. China has become the world's factory and garnered great wealth and, apparently, its military modernisation has reached a point that it felt confident to propose, a year or so ago, division of the world's two great oceans – the Pacific and the Indian – between the United States and itself! However, in its rise, China has, so far, offered no concept, not even in broad outline, of a framework of Asian cooperation for peace and security, not to speak of a new World Order to replace the existing international system comprising a network of global institutions, which the US had created in the twentieth century. Nor has China enunciated a new political philosophy or code of international conduct to match the great ideas, which originated in the US and have become the political currency of our time – liberty and freedom, dignity of man, human rights, sovereign equality of nations, democratic governance, market economy and globalisation.

Admittedly, the existing international system is in need of reform to bring it in line with the changing world politics, and it was expected that as the leading Asian power, China would help guide the process of change in the right direction. But, while seeking enhancement of its own role in global institutions, China has blocked the process by opposing the UN Security Council's (UNSC) permanent membership for India and Japan and the moves for elimination of the obnoxious veto vested in the five permanent members. Moreover, within Asia, China seems to spurn the rights, interests and sensitivities of its smaller neighbours. Because of its assertive claims on lands and seas on its periphery, concerns are felt in most Asian countries about peace and stability in Asia.

No one grudges China its rise to power and prosperity, but no Asian country, big or small, relishes the prospect of returning to a system of tributary states under a Middle Kingdom hegemon. Of course, China, with its millennial civilisation, its long history and the accumulated wisdom of centuries has the potential for accommodative, creative and cooperative leadership role expected of a modern great power, and China may rise to such a role at some stage. But for the present it seems more likely that the defining role in the twenty-first century will belong to the United States of America.

This view was contested by several participants in the ORF's in-house discussion. While acknowledging that since the vast Asian continent impinges on the rest of the world, a balanced, stable, peaceful and progressive Asia might be unattainable without wider, cooperative participation in Asian affairs, they expressed skepticism about the United States' ability to play any kind of a defining role in view of the critical economic problems it faces at home – the large debt, huge budget deficit, high unemployment and the increasing polarisation in the country's politics. Economic downturn in the US (and in Europe) since 2008 is a reality, which must not be overlooked. Several American writers are saying that their country is in terminal decline. Well-known American writer, Patrick Buchanan, is in despair about his country's future. In a recently published book, he is in doubt that America can survive till 2025. He questions whether the budget deficit of $1.15 trillion can be reduced. He thinks the government is helpless and there is a 'crisis of the system and the state itself'. This once-affluent country is deeply in China's debt, and its leaders are unabashedly asking for help from China (and India) to revive its faltering economy. In these circumstances, America's claims to continuing world leadership are unconvincing. Therefore, as another American writer, Martin Jacques has said, China will rule the world. Hopefully, the argument concluded, China will rule the world in partnership with India! This facetious hope was quickly quenched by a chorus of skeptical voices.

Our experts on US affairs intervened to say that speculation about America's decline is encouraged by the writings of the declinists among the American intellectual elite, a sensitive lot ready to pronounce doom at the slightest dent in the country's domestic solidity or a seeming challenge to its global stature. Even Henry Kissinger, one of the twentieth century's intellectual giants, writing in 1961 had lamented the decline America had suffered, according to him, since the end of the Second World War! An obtuse observation which not many took seriously, for that precisely was the period when American values and American hard and soft power were receiving worldwide acclaim. In 1987, three years before America's victory in the Cold War and the Soviet Union's disintegration, the eminent historian Paul Kennedy was forecasting America's impending decline because of its 'imperial overstretch'. Overstretch, yes; but the United States remains the world's unrivalled military power – even China acknowledges that – and still the most liberal donor of aid to developing countries. It is the first country to reach out with help to far-away lands affected by natural disasters.

Yes, there are these declinist narratives about America, the argument proceeded, and there is some basis for them too – excessive dependence on cheap imports in replacement of domestic manufacturing, money speculation and the profligacy of the Wall Street bankers, the housing bubble, and the squandering of national wealth and strength in avoidable wars. All these have taken a heavy toll on the American economy. But a lot of heart-searching is going on in America's open society, and corrective policy measures are being put in place. With the exit from Iraq and the planned winding up of the war in Afghanistan, the country can be expected to emerge from this miasmatic state within this decade, with its naturally endowed optimism, bounce and drive. America's recovery is ensured by its innate strengths – its sturdy and time-tested institutions, its vast reservoir of resources, its unmatched proficiency in science and technology, its large youthful and innovative population, and the diverse inherent capacities of its democratic system to redress its flaws and failures. Great new advances in American science and technology are on the anvil, which will revolutionise American manufacturing leading to unprecedented growth and prosperity. Like Ambassador Ako Kawato, I too believe, one of our US protagonists asserted, that 'AMERICA 2.0' is close at hand. At any rate, the US, despite its problems, is the most stable and prosperous country in the world. The conditions within China are so different! Immolations in Tibet, unending unrest in Xinjiang, a large section of the population still living in poverty and the rising frequency of protests and violence all over the country.

And, the argument proceeded: While China remains embroiled in quarrels over territory with major Asian powers, like Japan and India, and engages in bellicose rhetoric and militarily threatening behaviour towards its smaller neighbours, the initiative in diplomacy, the engine for maintaining peace and stability in a region in ferment, remains with the United States, which is busy reinforcing old ties and forging strategic partnerships with new friends in Asia. The US will, therefore, lead Asia and play the decisive role in shaping the Asian Century.

These concluding remarks were hotly contested by some on the ground that a country which is not even part of Asia geographically, could not possibly be a major player in reshaping Asian relations and the Asian Century.

At this juncture, I intervened to say that the world of the twenty-first century is a smaller, more intimate and interactive place than the world of even the last quarter of the twentieth century and that even in such a world the United States still is the only power with a global reach. It has proclaimed itself a Pacific Power. And it has interests and a presence, in one form or another, in every region of Asia's great landmass and in the Indian Ocean. I then suggested that our scholars specialising in different regions of Asia, should take a close look at the nature, scope, extent and quality of America's engagement in their respective areas of research. Their findings will not only help us decide which power – China or the US – will have the lead role in shaping the twenty-first century, but also suggest some guidelines for India's foreign policy. Non-alignment, I said, was a good policy in the early decades of independence. 'NON-ALIGNMENT 2.0' will not serve India's national interest in the world politics of the twenty-first century, and the new driving mantra for India's foreign policy should be All-around Engagement in pursuit of India's national interest in a calm and cooperative Asia, with special emphasis on engagement and cooperation with both China and the United States of America.

The suggestion was readily accepted; and this book is the result. This is by no means an exhaustive study of the subject, but it does highlight the astonishing ubiquity of American presence in all of Asia. Washington's policies and actions are, therefore, bound to exert a transformative influence on Asian developments.

Prof. Kesavan, a distinguished fellow at ORF, draws attention to the presence of 45,500 US troops in Japan and another 30,000 in South Korea and the stabilising influence American security alliances with Japan, South Korea, the Philippines, Singapore and Australia have on the security of the region without detriment to Washington's relations with Beijing. He points out that despite differences over Taiwan, Iran and Syria, currency issues, Intellectual Property Rights, climate change and China's maritime claims, the United States continues to seek a comprehensive framework of cooperation with China, its biggest trade partner in Asia. The Association of Southeast Asian Nations (ASEAN) find US engagement with them reassuring and have extended a quiet welcome to Washington's Asia pivot.

C. Raja Mohan, a well-known author and columnist and head of Strategic Studies at ORF, writes about the United States' rapidly improving political and security cooperation with Vietnam, India and Myanmar. Despite current tensions because of differences over Afghanistan and the Taliban havens in Pakistan, the US remains in a tolerant and enduring posture of engagement to sustain that country. Significantly, Afghanistan has recently entered into a strategic partnership with the United States.

Saeed Naqvi, a distinguished fellow at ORF, with his extensive knowledge of the situation in Afghanistan, is not convinced that the US forces will leave Afghanistan completely in 2014. He gives us many rare insights into the happenings in Afghanistan, their international repercussions and some interesting scenarios of Afghanistan's future. Naqvi's intimate knowledge of the Muslim world's history lends depth and a near-prophetic authority to his forecasts of developments in that region.

Uma Purushothaman, an Associate Fellow at ORF, considers the American role in the Arab world helpful in the region's transition to democracy and that in view of the enduring nature of its security and other interests, the US has no option but to remain engaged in the region. The Gulf countries, other than Iran, are heavily dependent on the United States. Along with Saudi Arabia, they are supportive of the large US naval base in Bahrain as also of the continuing US pressure and engagement in the Arab region.

Angira Sen Sarma, a scholar who has done a great deal of work in Central Asia, believes the Afghanistan crisis, energy and geopolitics will ensure long-term US engagement with the Central Asian Republics. Some Central Asian countries have willingly offered bases and transit facilities for American military operations in Afghanistan. All of them, including Russia, favour the continuing presence of American forces in Afghanistan.

Washington's ham-handed dealings with Russia are the only negative element in the pervasive sense of ease about the United States' presence in all regions of Asia and its active participation in Asian affairs. But, as Ajish P. Joy, an Associate Fellow at ORF, argues, though the US has been riding roughshod on Moscow's sensitivities, the two powers have worked together through comprehensive engagement to achieve solid results in arms control issues, Strategic Arms Reduction Talks (START) negotiations, missile deployment and on issues related to Afghanistan and Iran.

The conclusion that emerges from this study is that the US has a very large Asian presence, which is generally regarded as benign and beneficial in character, and is welcomed everywhere – quietly in some places and with enthusiasm in others.

The shift of power in the Asia Pacific caused by China's rapid rise has led to security-related uncertainties, and big and small Asian countries are seeking a balanced political and military environment through partnerships and alliances with the only other major power around – the United States of America. The parallel is not exact but the Asian scene is not much different from the European situation before the First World War except that the US had no presence in Europe then and the continent drifted into two calamitous wars. Since the United States' active involvement in European affairs after the Second World War, the spirit of cooperation, peace and harmony has reigned in that continent.

Historically, a time of rising powers is replete with tensions and unanticipated and potentially dangerous occurrences. America's presence in Asia, especially its balanced relations with other major Asian powers – China, India, Indonesia, Japan and Russia – will be a catalyst of stability and peace in the 'Asian Century'. Moreover, the future in the modern world will belong to a country that is most advanced in science and technology. In those two critical assets, which define power in our time, the United States is decades ahead of China, India and even Japan. Truly therefore, the twenty-first century may turn out to be America's Century in Asia just as the twentieth was America's Century in Europe.

I want to thank my colleagues for their contributions and the time and effort they invested in this enquiry – K.V. Kesavan, Uma Purushothaman, K. Yhome, C. Raja Mohan, Saeed Naqvi, Angira Sen Sarma and Ajish P. Joy. I owe thanks also to Nandan Unnikrishnan, vice president at ORF, who was good enough to vet the first draft of the manuscript. I owe an additional word of appreciation to Uma, who valiantly offered to write two chapters and helped me in preparing the manuscript for publication.

New Delhi
December 2012 Maharajakrishna Rasgotra

The United States in Northeast Asia

K. V. Kesavan

After the end of the Cold War and with the rise of China as an economic and military power, Northeast Asia has acquired much greater economic and strategic salience. The United States, though considered an outside power by some, has a strong presence in the region and has been deeply involved in its economic and security dynamics. Today, three of America's major trading partners – China, Japan and South Korea – are from this region. Until recently, Japan enjoyed the position as the region's biggest trading and investing partner of the US. But now China's total trade with the US has surpassed Japan's. In 2011, US-China trade amounted to $502 billion, whereas US trade with Japan and South Korea accounted for $295 billion and $100 billion, respectively.

American security interests in the region are old and deep, going back to the early years of the Cold War. The Korean War, the Taiwan issue and the Allied Occupation of Japan inevitably brought the region into the vortex of the Cold War politics and in the ensuing East-West rivalry, the US fashioned a network of security treaties with several Asian countries including Japan and South Korea. Even after the end of the Cold War, military alliances with Japan and South Korea have continued with new perspectives appropriate to the unfolding post-Cold War strategic milieu. Northeast Asia is one region where the legacies of the Cold War continue even now. Today, there are 47,000 US troops stationed in Japan and 28,000 troops in South Korea. The US has a strong military relationship with Taiwan.

The countries of the region share many common concerns on issues such as maritime security, energy, climate change and nuclear non-proliferation. Despite the enormous scope that these issues provide for regional cooperation, no tangible result has been achieved so far on the ground. On the contrary, they compete with one another to promote their own national interests. The fierce contest between China and Japan to exploit the natural resources that are supposed to lie in the East China Sea has not yet been resolved despite the opportunity that exists for both countries to jointly cooperate to exploit those resources.

An analysis of President Barack Obama's policies in the region needs to be prefaced by a brief look at the policies earlier adopted by President George W. Bush during his two terms from 2000 to 2008. Since his administration was deeply involved in anti-terrorism military campaigns in Afghanistan and later in Iraq, he could not devote as much time and interest to Northeast Asia as he would perhaps have wanted to. This had even aroused criticism that he was neglecting the region due to his obsession with Iraq and Afghanistan. But one important aspect of his East Asian policy should be seen in the close equation he was able to develop with Japan. Fortunately for President Bush, there was political stability in Japan during 2001-06 largely due to the strong leadership exercised by Koizumi Junichiro. Koizumi's consistent support to American policies both in Afghanistan and Iraq contributed a great deal to the strength of the bilateral security alliance, but within Japan, public opinion was sharply divided. In an effort to avoid the 1990-92 criticism of Japan as a country that only believed in checkbook diplomacy and was reluctant to take tangible measures as an ally, Koizumi's government passed several measures such as anti-terrorism act and extension of refuelling services to the Allies in the Indian Ocean area, which were lauded by the Bush administration. But Koizumi's uncritical support to the US on a range of issues created deep fissures within Japanese political circles. There were complaints in Japan that no other Japanese prime minister in recent years had gone so far to support the unpopular policies of the US president.

Further, Koizumi's regular visits to the controversial Yasukuni Shrine during his tenure had created unprecedented bitterness in Sino-Japanese relations. China's mounting trade and investment links with the US, Bush's compliments to China's diplomatic skills in handling North Korea and its nuclear policies, his decision to remove North Korea from the list of terrorist states, and his diminishing concern for the abduction issue created a great deal of discomfort and concern in Japan. But, by and large, the US administration under President Bush considered its alliance with Japan as the key element in its approach to the East Asian region, and part of the reason for this was to be seen in the close personal equations that Bush was able to maintain with Koizumi. Even so, there were many in the foreign policy establishment who were worried about Bush's penchant for unilateralism in making decisions on matters concerning Japan and Northeast Asia. For instance, information regarding Bush's decision to remove North

Korea from the list of terrorist states was reportedly communicated to Japan only at the last moment.[1]

The new administration under President Obama seemed to have had a good start as far as its relations with Japan were concerned. To be sure, since Japan itself did not figure prominently in the presidential campaign, it was rather difficult to figure out what the new administration would do after Obama's victory in the elections. This feeling was all the stronger in Japan where many thought that a Democratic administration might raise protectionist barriers against Japanese goods. Further, Japanese political and business leaders had not forgotten the two terms of President Bill Clinton's administration, when they had enough reasons to fear that Washington was shifting its focus of interest from Japan to China. Many were reminded of President Bill Clinton's 'Japan passing' days in the 1990s.

The decision of the new Secretary of State Hillary Clinton to start her first overseas trip with Japan seems to have given the Japanese considerable satisfaction. They believed that her tenure had started on the right note. Symbolism apart, one of the main objectives of Clinton's visit was to assure Japan that the bilateral security alliance between Washington and Tokyo would continue to be the 'cornerstone' of US foreign policy in Asia.[2] She asserted that there was no question of shifting America's priorities from Japan to any other country since the alliance 'is a solid, tested and enduring source of cooperation'. She believed that it would be difficult to imagine addressing many of the global challenges including global recession, climate change, terrorism, nuclear proliferation, maritime security and energy cooperation without stable US-Japan cooperation. Clinton took the unprecedented step of meeting the leaders of the Opposition Democratic Party, including Ichiro Ozawa, in the belief that the alliance should continue to enjoy bipartisan support, even if a political change were to occur in Japan. On China, she allayed Japanese concerns by stating that 'Our relationship with China is still developing as is Japan's relationship with China. So it is important that we focus on it and that we pay attention and try to figure out how we are going to work out the way of cooperation with China.'[3]

As part of further cementing the security partnership, Clinton and her then Japanese counterpart Nakasone Hirofumi signed an agreement for relocating 8,000 US Marine Corps along with their family members (numbering about 9,000) based in Okinawa, to Guam. This was part of an earlier agreement signed in 2006 between the two countries with the objective of bringing relief to the Okinawa people without, in any way, reducing the level of deterrence in the region. Japan agreed to provide $6.09 billion out of a total of $10.27 billion for the realignment of the US Forces.[4]

The Japanese were also quite anxious to know from Clinton more about the Obama administration's policy on denuclearisation of North Korea as well as on the question of Japanese abductees. During the closing stages of the Bush administration, many Japanese suspected Washington of going rather soft on the Pyongyang regime by removing it from the list of terrorist states. In response, Clinton assured the Japanese that the abduction issue was a part of the 'six-party talks'. In an attempt to allay Japanese concerns, she not only met several relatives of the abductees, but also urged North Korea to stop its nuclear and missile programmes and show greater responsibility on the question of abduction.[5]

It is interesting to note how on the eve of the secretary of state's visit, both Japan and South Korea showed anxiety to coordinate their positions on how to respond to the new US administration. Both had common concerns on the conduct and course of US diplomacy in East Asia. Japanese Foreign Minister

Hirofumi Nakasone visited Seoul on 11 February 2008, to meet his South Korean counterpart Yu Myung-hwan to formulate common approaches to the Obama administration. Criticising North Korea for heightening tensions in the region, both urged it to conduct itself in a manner that would contribute to peace and stability in East Asia.

Political Change from the LDP to the DPJ–Led Administration in Japan

It is also important to note how a major political change in Japan from a Liberal Democratic Party (LDP)-led coalition to a Democratic Party of Japan (DPJ)-led coalition administration initially created problems of adjustment for both countries. Following a massive victory in the August 2009 Lower House election, the DPJ came to power on a plank of assurances to bring about changes in the political, economic and diplomatic spheres. In the field of foreign policy, it promised to maintain the security alliance with the US on the basis of 'independence and equality'. In tune with this promise, the DPJ terminated Japan's extension of refuelling services to the Allied Forces in the Indian Ocean in January 2010. But its attempts to have the Futenma marine air base shifted to another place outside the Okinawa Islands not only ended in a miserable failure, but also led to the resignation of Prime Minister Hatoyama Yukio. The US government stood firmly by the terms of the 2006 agreement, which stipulates that the base could be shifted to another suitable site but within the islands.

In the third week of October 2009, US defence Secretary Robert Gates visited Japan to broach the subject with the government leaders. While he sounded 'sympathetic to the realignment plan' of the DPJ government, he candidly told the Japanese leaders that the relocation of Futenma to any place outside the island would be 'politically untenable and operationally unworkable'.[6] Recalling the long and vexatious negotiations that ultimately led to the 2006 agreement, he advised that it would be in their best interest to go ahead with the agreement, which he described as the only viable proposition. In response to Gates's exhortation, Japanese Foreign Minister Okada Katsuya explained the changes that had taken place in Japanese politics. In particular, he mentioned how in all four electoral constituencies in Okinawa, candidates opposed to the 2006 agreement had been elected in the August 2009 election. Subsequently, it turned out that the prime minister was badly caught in a crossfire between the stubbornness of the US stand that made relocation of the base outside Okinawa impossible and the growing discontent of the Okinawans. The final decision that came in a US-Japan joint statement in May 2010 clearly stated that the Futenma base would be shifted from its present location to a sparsely populated place in Schwab within Okinawa.[7] From the beginning Hatoyama failed to correctly understand the position of the US on relocation and the final decision that the Futenma base would be transferred to another place, within the islands, seriously compromised his stand and there was no alternative for him except to step down as prime minister.

The new government headed by Kan Naoto was more realistic in accepting what the US wanted on the question of base relocation and showed strong inclination to promote friendly relations with the US in other spheres as well. In his policy speech delivered in the Japanese Diet on 11 June 2010, he endorsed that he would undertake in a thorough manner a reduction of the burden on Okinawa in line with the Japan-US agreement reached at the end of May. He expressed his full support to the bilateral security alliance in glowing terms, 'The Japan-US alliance can be said to be an internationally shared asset in that it supports not only the defence of Japan, but also the stability and prosperity of Asia and the Pacific region. I will continue to deepen our alliance steadily.'[8]

Given the complex nature of the Futenma base issue, both countries acted wisely to make efforts to work towards achieving the larger goals of the alliance. This could be done by reiterating and redefining the strategic objectives of the alliance. But before they could do so, the DPJ's debacle in the House of Councillors' election held in July 2010 was a serious set-back that created problems for the Japanese government in the legislative processes. More than that, what seemed to have weakened Kan's position was his estranged relations with the party's strategist and strong man Ozawa Ichiro. Much of his time was spent in addressing the internal party squabbles rather than concentrating on several domestic and foreign policy questions. When the triple tragedy – earthquake, tsunami and nuclear crisis occurred on 11 March 2011, the Kan government was found totally ill-prepared to face it. It was under such circumstances that the US showed its readiness to help Japan in the whole process of recovery and reconstruction. Operation Tomadachi, which witnessed a massive support system put into action by the US military forces clearly underlined what Prime Minster Kan called the depth of their *kizuna* (bond). The US deployed its aircraft carrier *Ronald Reagan* as well as hundreds of its military personnel to rush relief measures to the disaster-affected areas. President Obama said, 'The Japanese people are not alone in this time of great trial and sorrow. Across the Pacific, they will find a hand of support extended from the United States as they get back on their feet.'[9]

An important meeting between Obama and Kan was held at the time of the Group of Eight (G-8) meeting in Deauville,

France, on 26 May 2011, and they clearly expressed how they shared many security concerns on a number of global and regional issues. Both agreed to make serious efforts to achieve progress on the Futenma base issue. Obama pledged that the US would work closely with Japan on the changing political situation in the Middle East and coordinate with Japan in dealing with Iran. In return, Kan assured Obama of Japan's cooperation with US policies in Afghanistan and Pakistan. On North Korea, both agreed on its denuclearisation and the need to reopen the six-party talks and to seek a solution to the abduction issue.[10] On 3 June, both defence Secretary Robert Gates and his Japanese counterpart Kitazawa Toshimi met on the margins of the Shangri-La Dialogue in Singapore to reiterate their commitment to the relocation plan for the Futenma base on the Okinawa Islands.[11]

These developments convinced both the US and Japan of the need to convene a meeting of the bilateral Security Consultative Committee (2+2) to carry forward their security discussions. The committee which met on 21 June issued a joint statement and three other documents pertaining to bilateral cooperation in response to the 11 March Fukushima catastrophe, progress on the realignment of US forces in Japan and the host nation support.

In the preamble itself, the joint statement referred to the close collaboration between the two governments in the aftermath of the March 11 earthquake, tsunami and nuclear emergency and how it had given renewed confidence to the alliance and deepened the friendship between the two countries.[12] The joint statement spelt out a long list of common strategic objectives that would bind them together: ensuring the security of Japan and strengthening peace and stability in the Asia-Pacific region; enhancing the capability to address a variety of contingencies affecting the US and Japan; achieving complete and verifiable denuclearisation of North Korea; strengthening trilateral security and defence cooperation with both Australia and the Republic of South Korea; encouraging China's responsible and constructive role in regional stability and prosperity, its cooperation on global issues and its adherence to international norms of behaviour; encouraging the peaceful resolution of Cross-Strait issues through dialogue; encouraging Russia's constructive engagement in the Asia Pacific region including a peaceful resolution of the territorial question between Russia and Japan; maintaining maritime security; preventing and eradicating terrorism; strengthening security cooperation among the US, Japan and ASEAN; welcoming India as a strong and enduring Asia-Pacific partner and encouraging India's growing engagement with the region and participation in regional architecture and promoting trilateral dialogue among the US, Japan and India; maintaining freedom of navigation; strengthening international cooperation on disaster prevention and relief.[13]

It was further recognised that the overarching convergence of their security interests could be clearly seen in two major developments in the year 2010.The new National defence Program Guidelines (NDPG) formulated by the DPJ government underline the need to build a 'dynamic defence force' that is marked by 'enhanced mobility, flexibility, sustainability, and versatility'. The guidelines reinforce the commitment made by the US in its 2010 Quadrennial defence Review to strengthen deterrence and maintain and enhance its military presence in the Asia Pacific region to address such challenges as the proliferation of nuclear and ballistic missile technologies, anti-access and area denial capabilities and other threats to outer space, high seas and cyberspace.[14] Taking into consideration the above security strategies, the two have sought to specify many areas where the alliance could be further strengthened.

Several important official meetings and visits soon followed, which served to further consolidate the trends towards better bilateral understanding. In August 2011, US Vice President Joseph R. Biden visited Japan and made a strong impression on the Japanese people. Evincing keen interest in the execution of the rehabilitation measures, he visited the disaster affected areas in the Miyagi Prefecture and assured Japan of the continued US support to all rehabilitation measures.[15] Shortly thereafter, Prime Minister Kan demitted his office and his successor Noda Yoshihiko lost no time in registering his gratitude to the US government for its massive assistance programme.

Taking advantage of his visit to the UN session in September, Noda had his first summit meeting with President Obama where he emphasised the importance of the bilateral security partnership 'which has become more unwavering since the 11 March Fukushima tragedy'.[16] Further, in his first policy speech at the Diet, Noda also made positive references to the US-Japan security alliance. In addition, he assured Obama that his government would soon take a decision on its position on the Trans-Pacific Partnership (TPP) free trade pact.

President Obama subsequently gave a new thrust to his broader Asia-Pacific policy by supporting the key regional organisations like the Asia-Pacific Economic Cooperation (APEC) and the East Asia Summit (EAS). First, he hosted the meeting of the APEC in Hawaii in September 2011. He followed it up by visiting Australia, where he underscored his administration's commitment to the Australia, New Zealand, United States Security Treaty (ANZUS). Further, he and Australian Prime Minister Julia Gillard decided to station a small number of US military personnel in Darwin. But a more significant development was the participation of the US in the annual EAS, where Obama clearly expressed America's desire to see the EAS develop more interest in political and security questions. He even suggested that maritime security and nuclear non-proliferation should initially draw the attention of the EAS.[17] Expectedly, China did not agree with this and maintained that questions like the maritime territorial issues should at best be discussed bilaterally between aggrieved countries and not in multilateral forums. Another important aspect of Obama's policy concerned the American interest in seeking to open new channels of communication with Myanmar. Obama sent Secretary of State Hillary Clinton to Myanmar in November 2011 and this had an immediate effect on Japan, which also sent its Foreign Minister Gemba Koichiro to Yangon in the last week of December 2011. This was the first visit by a Japanese Foreign minister in nine years. During his two-day visit, he met the top leaders of the Myanmar government to discuss the process of democratisation in the country. Expressing his country's readiness to extend economic cooperation to Myanmar, Gemba discussed the question of signing an investment agreement with Yangon and also Tokyo's interest in the development of the Tarawa port as part of Japan's interest in carrying out a comprehensive development of Myanmar.[18]

US-South Korea Security Partnership

One important aspect of President Obama's Asia policy is to work closely with, and extend full support to, those countries that have maintained security alliances with the US like Japan, South Korea, the Philippines and Australia. Obama considers South Korea's role to be very critical in the maintenance of peace and order in the region. In June 2009, Obama and South Korean President Lee Myung-bak signed the 'Joint Vision for Alliance of the United States of America and the Republic of

Korea' by which both leaders pledged to build a 'comprehensive strategic alliance of bilateral, regional and global scope based on common values and mutual trust'.[19] The US pledged to continue to provide extended deterrence to South Korea including its nuclear umbrella. Both the US and South Korea pledged to ensure the complete and verifiable elimination of North Korea's nuclear weapons and ballistic missile development programmes and promote respect for the human rights of the people of North Korea. The US considers that Pyongyang's nuclear weapons and missile technology development programmes constitute a grave threat not only to Japan and South Korea, but also to the various efforts made by the US to prevent proliferation of weapons of mass destruction.

President Obama was quite pleased to see South Korea joining the Proliferation Security Initiative (PSI). In October 2010, the two countries signed the 'Strategic Alliance 2015' containing a number of strategic planning guidelines to formulate new strategic plans for countering threats from North Korea.[20] On 23 November 2010, the US extended strong support to South Korea by condemning North Korea for bombing Yeonpyeong Island, a civilian populated South Korean island.[21] The bombing killed two South Korean soldiers and wounded 14 people. A similar North Korean attack on a South Korean warship that killed 46 sailors in March 2010 had also elicited a strong warning from the US.[22] The Obama administration has shown its keenness to consult Japan and South Korea in formulating a unified stand against North Korea. In December 2009 a trilateral meeting of the Foreign ministers took place in Washington and this was followed by another such meeting in Hawaii in November 2010. They agreed to consult each other on the question of how to respond to North Korea's challenges in different spheres. They strongly criticised North

Korea's proposed construction of uranium enrichment facilities in violation of the UN Security Council (UNSC) resolutions 1718 and 1874 as well as Pyongyang's own commitments under the 2005 joint communiqué of the six-party talks.

The US and China

The Obama administration has shown great circumspection in the conduct of its policies towards China. It realises that peace and security in East Asia cannot be underwritten without the support and goodwill of China. It is therefore essential to build a comprehensive cooperative framework with China. It believes that efforts should be taken to make China a responsible stakeholder in the region. In addition, there are compelling reasons for the US to avoid confrontation with China. For one thing, China is the biggest Asian trading partner of the US. China's rapidly expanding market is throwing up unlimited opportunities for the US economy. China also holds the highest volume of US official bonds. One of the earliest steps that the Obama government took was to upgrade the US-China bilateral partnership into the US-China Strategic and Economic Dialogue (S&ED). Further, being a permanent member of the UNSC, China has enormous clout in the global diplomatic sphere. But at the same time, the US is very anxious that China does not emerge as a hegemon in the East Asian region. China's military power, particularly its naval strength, has expanded in recent years and how Beijing will project its military muscle in the region in the coming years will be a question of deep concern for Japan, South Korea and ASEAN countries. Secretary Hillary Clinton's statement at the ASEAN Regional Forum meeting held in Hanoi in 2010 about America's concern to preserve freedom of navigation in the South China Sea area was a clear message sent to China.[23] Similarly, Clinton's clarification that the US has an obligation to support Japan in the event of a conflict with China involving the Senkaku Islands was a clear warning to China that the US would stand by its traditional ally in defending the Islands.[24] Further, America's renewed enthusiasm to participate in many regional bodies like the EAS is indicative of its policy of hedging against the expanding influence of China. The US believes in a policy of engaging China, while simultaneously taking measures to hedge against China's attempts to wield undue influence in the region. In other words, as Prof. Gerald Curtis states, the US believes that reliance on Chinese goodwill and benign intentions is 'as ill-advised as assuming that China inevitably poses a major threat.'[25]

Conclusion

While the Obama administration has not drastically departed from the policies of the previous Republican administration, it has shown a strong inclination to avoid pursuing unilateralism in its diplomatic decisions. It has tended to strongly support its traditional allies like Japan, South Korea and Australia and fostered mutual consultations with them. Even when the Obama administration had serious differences with the newly elected DPJ government under Hatoyama Yukio on the Futenma military base issue, there was awareness on both sides of the enduring nature of their relationship and the strategic necessity of the continuation of a strong American presence in Japan in the interests of stability and peace in the region. Both sides understood the realities on the ground and recognised the mutual security alliance as the cornerstone of their present and future foreign policies. Clearly, the US will maintain its strong presence in Northeast Asia, which will continue to be an important factor in the region's peace and stability.

The US-China Engagement

Uma Purushothaman

The US-China bilateral relationship is one of the most important in the world, one which will define the course of international relations in the 21st century. Dealing with China has become the pre-eminent foreign policy challenge for the US today. Over the last few decades, the US-China relationship has seen highs as well as lows. It is a very complex and complicated relationship, in which there are elements of both cooperation and conflict. While on the one hand, both countries are interdependent particularly because of trade, on the other, each views the other with suspicion.

Over the last one year, there has certainly been a reorientation of US foreign policy towards Asia in general. This was spelled out in Secretary of State Hillary Clinton's article 'America's Pacific Century' in *Foreign Policy* in November 2011, where she argued that one of the important tasks for America after its withdrawal from Iraq and Afghanistan would be to increase its diplomatic, economic and strategic investment in the Asia-Pacific region, which she describes as a 'key driver of global politics'. Again, in its defence Strategic Guidelines released in January 2012, the Pentagon declared that the US would 'of necessity rebalance toward the Asia Pacific region' to protect its economic and security interests.[1] This rebalancing involves the strengthening of ties with the United States' Asian allies, high-level visits to the region and expanding cooperation with new partners.

President Obama has also said that he wants the US to re-establish its leadership role in Asia. All of this has been termed as the 'US pivot to Asia' by scholars. The US has joined the EAS, institutionalising Washington's role in the region. China views the US pivot to Asia as a strategy that is aimed at containing it. Hillary Clinton in a statement to the Senate Foreign Relations Committee said, 'We are in a competition for influence with China,' and she went on to add, 'let's put aside the humanitarian, do-good side of what we believe in. Let's just talk straight realpolitik. We are in competition with China.' It is in this context that US-China relations become important. This paper lists out and analyses the current issues in US-China relations from the US perspective.

Trade and Economic Relations

One of the most important areas of engagement between China and the US is trade. The Chinese and American economies are extremely interdependent. This economic and trade relationship is mutually beneficial. US-China trade increased from $2 billion in 1979 to over $460 billion in 2011[2] and China is now the US' second-largest trading partner, third-largest export market and biggest source of imports.[3] On the other hand, the US is

China's biggest market and an important source of Foreign Direct Investment (FDI). China is an important market for the US due to its rapid economic growth and large population and has been the fastest-growing export market for the US over the last ten years. Besides, many American firms use inexpensive Chinese components or assemble their products in China, making their goods cheaper and more competitive. Also, China's policy of buying US treasury securities has helped the US to keep domestic interest rates low; it currently holds over $1.15 trillion in US treasury bonds though it has recently reduced its holdings of American debt. Thus, while China depends on the US for foreign investments for its own economic growth, the US depends on China to hold its sovereign debt.

Despite this interdependence and mutually beneficial trade ties, the US and China have many differences over economic issues, which have been exacerbated by the impact of the recession in the US and the fact that China was comparatively less affected by the recession. China's emergence as the second-largest economy in the world and the largest holder of US treasury bonds and US debt has caused concern in the US. While the US has the largest trade deficit in the world, China has the largest trade surplus. Also, China runs a huge bilateral trade surplus with the US, of US$295.45 billion in 2011,[4] and this has become another source of friction in relations.

Unlike other currencies, the Yuan is not market-based floating exchange rate and is pegged to the US dollar. The US feels that China's undervalued Yuan increases US trade deficit by helping Chinese exports. US trade deficit with China was around $273 billion in 2010 and hindered growth in US employment, an important domestic issue. This is because an undervalued Yuan makes Chinese exports to the world markets cheap and imports to China become more expensive, thus contributing to a global economic imbalance. The US feels that an appreciation in the Yuan's value would make US goods and services more competitive while at the same time halt outsourcing of American jobs.[5] Through much of 2011, the US focussed on appealing to China to stop devaluing the Yuan artificially and to consume more to reduce the imbalance in the global economy. China had agreed in June 2010 to revert to a 'managed float' foreign exchange regime for the Yuan. The US Senate even passed a trade bill in October 2011 to pressurise China into appreciating its currency.

China, on the other hand, was concerned about the US Federal Reserve's decision to pump in $600 billion into the US economy and denied that its currency was undervalued while accusing the US of trying to make it a scapegoat for global economic problems, which were caused by other countries. It felt that a revaluation of the Yuan would increase unemployment within China. It also called for an alternative for the US dollar as a reserve currency saying that growing US debt will cause inflation in the United States and lead to a sharp depreciation of the dollar, thus reducing the value of China's dollar holdings. Some policymakers in the US also feel that with China becoming the largest holder of US treasury securities, it could use this to put pressure on the US in bilateral and international issues.

Another trade-related dispute between the US and China relates to the latter not doing enough to protect Intellectual Property Rights (IPRs). The US has placed China in the 'priority watch list' of worst violators of IPRs. Other US grievances include China's domestic subsidies, interventions to promote state enterprises and its use of trade remedy laws to protect domestic industries. Among the other trade-related issues are China's export restrictions on several industrial raw materials which, the US argues, is against

World Trade Organization (WTO) laws, and the United States' push for a new free trade pact, the TPP, which excludes China. China sees the TPP as a counterweight to the ASEAN Plus Three grouping and feels that it infringes on its sphere of influence.[6] The US has accused China and other emerging economies of causing the stalemate at the Doha round of trade negotiations.

China, on the other hand, accuses the US of protectionism through the use of anti-dumping and anti-subsidy measures on Chinese products. It criticises the US for its high consumption rate, low savings rate, long-term debt and loose monetary policy.[7] China has also criticised the US Federal Reserve's quantitative easing policy. Its trade minister, Chen Deming, told a Chinese newspaper that 'uncontrolled printing of dollars and rising international prices for commodities are causing an imported inflationary "shock" for China and are a key factor behind increasing uncertainty'.[8] China is keen on reforming the global economic order so that it gets a bigger voice in decision-making in international financial institutions. The US has primacy in making and implementing rules in the global economic order and the US dollar is the currency used for global trade. As the second largest economy, China wants a bigger say in setting the international financial agenda.

Maritime Disputes

Maritime disputes between China and the US have arisen because of China's unhappiness with US military ships conducting surveillance and military activities in China's Exclusive Economic Zone (EEZ). The US, not being a party to the UNCLOS (UN Convention on the Law of the Sea), believes that it has the right to conduct such operations in China's EEZ without permission; China, a party to the UNCLOS, believes that the UNCLOS allows countries to limit military activities in their EEZs.[9] This difference in interpretations has led to many encounters between US naval ships and Chinese naval and fishing ships in China's EEZ. China opposed the US-South Korea joint exercises in the Yellow Sea in 2010, which were held in the aftermath of provocations by North Korea. China has become more assertive recently about its territorial claims on the South China Sea, Yellow Sea and East China Sea, based on irredentism.

The South China Sea has some of the busiest shipping lanes in the world and is seen as a source of seafood and hydrocarbons. Some scholars also argue that China's desire to assert its sovereignty over the semi-closed sea is because it is integral to its nuclear submarine and maritime strategy.[10] In the South China Sea, China claims sovereignty over the Paracel Islands, Spratlys, the entirely submerged Macclesfield Bank and the largely submerged Pratas, which are rich in fish and are also said to have oil and gas deposits. This has raised hackles in other countries, which have similar claims but do not have the hard power to back up their claims. These islands are claimed, in parts, by Brunei, Indonesia, Malaysia, the Philippines, and Vietnam, and in whole by Taiwan. In meetings with American officials and in public statements, China has asserted that it sees the South China Sea as part of its 'core interest'.[11]

Japan and China also have disputes related to maritime rights in the East China Sea. In the East China Sea, China claims sovereignty over the Senkaku (Diaoyu) Islands. However, China does not have administrative control over these islands unlike Japan, which has administered them since the 1972 Okinawa Reversion Agreement. Taiwan also claims these islands as part of its territory. It is believed that the waters surrounding these islands contain vast reserves of natural gas. In 2010, China and Japan had a showdown near the Senkaku (Diaoyu) Islands in the East China Sea. Following the detention of the crew of a Chinese fishing trawler that collided with the Japanese coast guard patrol boats in disputed waters, China stopped selling rare earths to Japan. During the stand-off, the US announced that in the event of a military conflict, it would uphold its commitment to Japan's security under the US-Japan Treaty of Mutual Cooperation and Security of 1960.

China also has staked claims over the Yellow Sea, the northern part of the East China Sea, which is a vital gateway to Beijing and separates China and South Korea. The US and South Korea conducted naval exercises in the Yellow Sea to warn North Korea after it sank a South Korean ship in March 2010, killing 46 sailors. China condemned the exercises because of its objection to military exercises off its coast and accused Washington and Seoul of heightening tensions in the Korean peninsula. It retaliated by conducting its own naval exercises in the Yellow Sea. It also conducted military drills along its Eastern coast.

These disputes have perhaps inevitably dragged in the US too for two reasons: 1) The US is a Pacific power and it needs to uphold the freedom of navigation; and 2) The countries with which China has disputes are either allies or countries with which the US is strengthening relations as part of its pivot to Asia. Moreover in 2009, the US accused Chinese naval ships of harassing an American surveillance ship off the island of Hainan. The US has, therefore, asserted its right to freedom of navigation and respect for international law in the South China Sea and said that it opposes the use of force by any claimant in the South China Sea.[12] Admiral Willard in his statement before the Senate Armed Services Committee in April 2011 observed that China's maritime behaviour is a growing concern and that in what it calls its 'near seas', China 'seek(s) to restrict or exclude foreign, in particular, US military, maritime and air activities'.[13] Hillary Clinton also said that the US has a 'national interest' in the South China Sea and it conducted naval exercises with Vietnam there, making it one of the potential fronts in a new US-China rivalry.[14] The US offered its help as a mediator; something to which China responded strongly saying the US was trying to 'internationalise' a regional dispute that should be solved by the parties concerned.[15]

The Chinese Foreign Minister declared secretary Clinton's statement as an attack on China and warned the US against making the South China Sea an international or multilateral issue.[16] The US has further strengthened its relations and held joint military exercises with the Philippines, which also claims part of the sea. Other than the US and the countries which claim territory in the Sea, sea-faring countries like Australia and India are also worried about China's intentions as the sea is a recognised international waterway.[17] Though tensions eased after China agreed to cooperate in drafting guidelines for a code of conduct with ASEAN countries, the myth of China's 'peaceful rise' has evaporated in the region and distrust of China's intentions remains high in the region.

America's Partners: Old and New

Many countries with whom China has historic disputes or disagreements are also allies and partners of the US. These alliances and partnerships have become stronger in recent years. These countries have moved closer to the US as they feel the US, unlike China, does not have any territorial ambitions in Asia. They see the US as a security hedge in case they have problems with China in the future. Moreover, they feel that the US rebalancing to Asia will add to regional stability. This has also aroused Chinese suspicions that these countries will be used to counter China in the region.

The Taiwan issue is one of the most complicated in US-China relations. Though the US follows the 'one China' policy, it maintains close economic and security ties with Taiwan and is Taiwan's foremost ally. China defines Taiwan as one of its 'core interests' and declares that it will integrate the island either peacefully or through force. In any case, it will not allow Taiwan to become independent. So its naval development has been concentrated on what military experts call 'anti-access', or 'area denial' (A2AD) capabilities to prevent the US from coming to Taiwan's help in case a conflict breaks out between Beijing and Taipei. Taiwan is 'the issue over which both sides (US and China) most actively continue to plan for the possibility of future military confrontation',[18] and is therefore a potentially dangerous issue. China has also stationed missiles on the coast opposite Taiwan in support of its claim over the island. Thus, despite growing economic ties, Cross-Straits relations continue to be tense.

US-Taiwan relations can be traced to the Chinese Civil War of the 1940s. During the Korean War, the US positioned its Seventh Fleet in the Taiwan Straits, cementing the bilateral relationship. Later the Mutual defence Treaty and the Formosa Resolution of 1955 became symbols of the growing economic, political and military engagement between the US and Taiwan. When President Carter decided to sever relations with Taiwan to normalise relations with China, the Congress responded by passing the Taiwan Relations Act of 1979. US support to Taiwan has been bolstered by the support that Taiwan enjoys on Capitol Hill. Thus, the US has had to play a delicate balancing act in managing its relations with China and Taiwan.

Under the Taiwan Relations Act of 1979, the US is obligated

to give arms to Taiwan to guarantee its security. Every time it does so, China reacts angrily as it feels that this emboldens those who call for Taiwan's independence and is therefore destabilising in nature. The US position is that these arms sales give Taiwan's leaders the confidence to engage with China's leadership. In 2010, China broke off military ties temporarily with the US in retaliation to US arms sales to Taiwan. Again in 2011, when the US provided Taiwan with one of its biggest arms deals worth $5.85 billion, China reacted angrily saying the deal undermined its core interests and would hurt its ties with the US. However, the US tried to take the edge off China's concerns by only agreeing to upgrade Taiwan's F-16s and refusing to sell new F-16 aircraft requested by Taiwan.

China eyes with suspicion USA's strengthened alliances and partnerships with neighboring countries like Japan, India, Vietnam and other Southeast Asian countries. The US-Japan alliance can be traced to the end of the Second World War when the two joined hands to work against the spread of Communism. The US' commitment to protect Japan assumes relevance in the context of the recent China-Japan stand-off over the disputed Senkaku (Diaoyu) Islands. Article 5 of the 1960 US-Japan Security Treaty commits the US to aid Japan in defending territory under Japanese administration. China is also Japan's largest trading partner and a major destination for Japanese investments. However, relations continue to be affected by historic animosity, territorial disputes and distrust of each other's intentions. This was most evident during the recent fishing boat dispute and China's subsequent decision to stop the export of rare earth metals to Japan.

India and the US have come closer to each other than ever before. Many Chinese experts believe that the bourgeoning US-India relationship is aimed at containing China, despite repeated assertions from Indian officials that this is not the case. India's unresolved problems with China, including the boundary dispute and Tibet, add to this feeling. The US has also started engaging on a stronger footing with the countries of Southeast Asia. The US has opened a dialogue with Myanmar and removed some of the sanctions imposed on it. Hillary Clinton's visit to Myanmar, the first by a US secretary of state since 1955, is public recognition of American appreciation for the reforms initiated by the regime in Myanmar. The US has significantly strengthened military ties with Vietnam, another neighbour with which China has disputes. Vietnam has accused the Chinese Navy of harassing Vietnamese fishermen who venture into waters that China claims, as well as cutting the cables of survey ships belonging to Petro Vietnam in the area. Vietnam retaliated by conducting live fire drills in the area to which China countered with naval exercises. In 2011, Washington and Hanoi even conducted joint naval exercises. This is important in the context of reports suggesting that China cut the cables of Vietnamese ships engaged in oil exploration in the South China Sea. The US also held naval exercises with the Philippines. It has expanded its training exercises to include Cambodia and Malaysia as well.

Human Rights and Tibet

Human rights in China has been an intractable issue for long in the US-China bilateral relationship. Major human rights issues on which the US criticised China recently were China's censorship of the Internet, its refusal to allow Nobel Peace Laureate Liu Xiaobo and his representatives to travel to Oslo for the award function and his subsequent imprisonment, of harassment of political dissidents and other adverse conditions prevailing in Xinjian and Tibet. A bilateral dialogue on human rights, which was held in May 2011 in the backdrop of an increased crackdown by China on dissidents amid fears of Arab Spring-like protests, led to no breakthrough. The US State Department brings out country report on human rights practices annually. On 8 April 2011, it released its report on China for the year 2010. The report criticised China for restrictions on freedom of religion, speech, assembly, internet and travel and use of torture in prisons.[19] It was particularly critical of China's record in Tibet and Hong Kong. China retorted by bringing out its own report titled 'The Human Rights Record of the United States in 2010'. The report criticised the US for violence in the country, violation of its citizens' civil and political rights, restrictions on the internet, lack of protection of social, economic and cultural rights, gender discrimination and racial discrimination.[20] Therefore, it said, the US has no right to judge other countries on their human rights record.

Tibet is a further stumbling block in Sino-US relations. China defines Tibet as a 'core interest'. Though the US recognises Tibet as a part of China, the US Congress has passed several resolutions about human rights abuses and the impact of Chinese rule on Tibet's religion and culture. President Obama's meetings with the Dalai Lama in 2010 and 2011, despite China's warning that such meetings would affect US-China relations, show that the US remains concerned about the situation in Tibet. The US has repeatedly asked the Chinese to resolve the Tibet issue through dialogue, an advice which the Chinese resent and continue to ignore. China's defence against the West's criticism has been that unlike the West, which defines human rights only as individual rights, China sees human rights as individual as well as collective rights. So the issue of human rights in US-China bilateral relations does not show any signs of going away.

Chinese Positions on Iran, Syria and North Korea

Sino-US relations have been tense due to China's positions on issues such as Syria, Iran and North Korea. The Obama administration has attempted to make non-proliferation a core area of cooperation with China, particularly with regard to Iran and North Korea. China has supported sanctions against both countries and even participated in the nuclear security summit in April 2010 despite US arms sales to Taiwan and Obama's meeting with the Dalai Lama.[21]

China has refused to toe the US line with regard to Iran's nuclear program. It has refused to impose bilateral sanctions on Iran unlike the US and the EU countries. Though it supported UN sanctions on Iran, it did so with the rider that the sanctions should not hurt the civilian population and the economy, and pushed for targeted sanctions. Moreover, a 2009 CIA report implicated some Chinese firms for helping Iran achieve self sufficiency in developing ballistic missiles.[22] China has invested heavily in Iranian oil and gas fields and is a major consumer of Iranian oil. After the US imposed fresh sanctions on Iran this year, China has been reducing its dependence on Iranian oil. Some US scholars allege that China supports Iran because it feels that a strong Iran, which has hostile relations with the US, would be in its interests as the US would be forced to keep large military forces in the Middle East, which would limit its ability to project force in East Asia, the region where China's core interests lie.[23]

China remains North Korea's closest ally. Modern relations between the two date back to the Korean War when China helped the North Koreans against the South Koreans who were supported by the Americans. China has actively participated in the six-party talks and supported UN sanctions against North

Korea. China has so far adopted a policy of engagement over confrontation with North Korea as it fears that the collapse of the North Korean regime might create a refugee problem in China and ultimately a unified Korea aligned to the US. China tried to shield North Korea from diplomatic repercussions for sinking the South Korean ship *Cheonan* and for shelling the South Korean island of Yeonpyeong.[24] The US, on the other hand, has tried to isolate North Korea internationally. Another issue of concern for the US is China's policy of repatriating refugees from North Korea back to that country. The recent deal reached between the US and Korea in which North Korea agreed to suspend some elements of its nuclear programme in return for food aid is a positive sign, which might well mean the resumption of the six-party talks. The deal has been welcomed by China and might pave the way for peace on the Korean peninsula.

Another issue that has put the US and China at loggerheads recently is the current situation in Syria. China, along with Russia, vetoed two UNSC resolutions backed by the US and its allies that condemned the Syrian regime for cracking down on opponents of the regime. Clearly, China does not want to be seen as being supportive of a resolution, like resolution 1973 on Libya, which was used by the West to intervene in Libya and bring down the Gadaffi regime. Essentially, these differences boil down to China's uneasiness with the Western concepts of 'humanitarian intervention' and 'responsibility to protect' given the fact that China believes non-interference in other countries' internal affairs to be the fundamental principle of international relations.

China's Military Modernisation

China's military modernisation has added a whole new dimension to how the US views China. Since 2000, Chinese military spending has increased at an annual average of 15 percent.[25] China has the largest standing army in the world. China's attempts to develop a stealth fighter jet and missiles that can hit moving targets in the sea are other examples of China's new-found military prowess. Some American scholars believe that this modernisation is aimed at limiting the freedom of movement of the US military in Asia, and will impede its ability to come to the rescue of its friends and allies when they face threats. China's military modernisation thus poses a direct threat to US military predominance in the Asia-Pacific. Admiral Robert Willard, head of US Pacific Command, told the Senate Armed Services Committee in April 2011 that 'the scope and pace of its modernisation without clarity on China's ultimate goals remains troubling.'[26]

At the same time, US defence spending is set to decline as mandatory spending on social security and domestic entitlement programmes increases. China's military modernisation has raised fears in countries with which it has maritime and boundary disputes, such as India, Vietnam, Brunei, etc. This has the potential to drive these countries into the arms of the US for protection or into soft alliances with the US and also prompt them to buy more arms and modernise their militaries too. This could lead to an arms race in the Asian continent. It also raises questions about the safety of shipping lanes and the security of US allies like South Korea and Japan. As the 2011 Annual Report of US-China Economic and Security Review Commission states: 'While the exact pace and scale of China's military modernisation effort and the intentions behind it remain opaque to the outside world, it is clear that China is acquiring specific means intended to counter US military capabilities and exploit US weaknesses'.[27] The 2010 Quadrennial defence Review also aired the same apprehensions:

'...China has shared only limited information about the pace, scope, and ultimate aims of its military modernisation programmes, raising a number of legitimate questions regarding its long-term intentions'. [28]

China-US Competition in Africa, Middle East and Latin America

As China's need for influence, markets and resources grows, it is expanding into newer territories such as Africa, the Middle East and Latin America. This brings it into conflict with the US. In Africa, China has overtaken the US as the continent's largest trading partner. It has more consulates in the continent than the US. It has expanded its economic ties in the continent through trade and investment as well as aid, particularly in infrastructure projects. It has also had no hesitation to engage with regimes that have been condemned for human rights violations, corruption or lack of democracy by the West, like Sudan or Zimbabwe. This has increased its political influence and soft power in these countries. China has thus offered an alternative to the Western model of development, showing that economic growth can take place under state-led Capitalism with strict control of political rights. This obviously clashes with the American idea of free market democracy. China also has unambiguous political goals in its engagement with Africa: While on the one hand it wants to reduce the number of countries that recognise Taiwan, on the other hand, it wants Africa's votes in international fora. It has succeeded to a great extent on both counts. China further sees Africa as a market for its arms though it does not yet have any bases. Its share of the conventional arms market in Sub-Saharan Africa is about 15 percent; the percentage for small arms and light weapons is even higher.[29] The US, on the other hand, has a military command dedicated to Africa, i.e., the United States Africa Command (AFRICOM), a base in Djibouti and a facility in Ethiopia for operating drones.

Another region of increasing competition is Latin America, which the US has traditionally regarded as its sphere of influence starting with the Monroe Doctrine. Like in Africa, China has expanded its economic and political influence in this region too. It has invested in oil in Brazil, Ecuador as well as Venezuela. Trade between China and Latin America has grown rapidly and China has become the largest export destination for Brazil, Chile, and Peru and the second largest export destination for Argentina, Costa Rica, and Cuba.[30] It has used the same strategy that it used in Africa with the goals also being the same. However, Chinese influence in an area so close to the US geographically has caused concern in the US, which feels that Chinese growing influence will prove inimical to its economic and political interest in the region. The Latin American countries see China as a driver of economic growth, source of investment and funding for infrastructure projects and humanitarian aid, potential market for Latin American goods and an ally in the international community.[31] In the Middle East too, China's political and economic influence is increasing. This has been dealt with in more detail in another chapter in this book. China's increasing engagement with and expanding interests in the regions in which American influence had been dominant seems to act as a provocation of sorts for the US to deepen its engagement with regimes and countries in China's periphery. Though these issues show divergence between Washington and Beijing, there are several issues on which they can and should cooperate.

Climate Change, Afghanistan, Terrorism

The world needs the US and China to work together on many global issues as they cannot be resolved without cooperation between Washington and Beijing. Climate change is an area where the US and China need to work together. The Durban summit saw China and the US, two of the world's biggest emitters of carbon, agree to cut emissions by 2020.

On Afghanistan, both US and China share an interest in a stable Afghanistan. Neither would want fundamentalist elements to use Afghanistan as a base to target either of them. China is concerned that the Uighur movement in Muslim-dominated Xinjiang Autonomous region in western China might get support from the Taliban. The 76-kilometre long border between the two countries causes concern with regard to the spread of Islamic extremism from Afghanistan. Moreover, China now has substantial economic interests in the country, particularly in mining, and is today the largest foreign investor in the country. Instability in Afghanistan threatens the security of Chinese investments in that country. China thus has vital interests in a stable Afghanistan.

Fighting terrorism is another issue on which Beijing and Washington share an interest. Beijing assured US of support in fighting terrorism after the 9/11 attacks and supported Resolution 1373 on the need to fight against terrorism. The two countries have had regular bilateral consultations on counter-terrorism, though cooperation admittedly remains 'limited' according to the US State Department. [32]

Conclusion

There are elements of both cooperation as well as competition in US-China relations, which are likely to remain tense, if not confrontational, in Asia. This situation would come about because of China's aspirations to increase its influence and the United States' reluctance to give up its primacy in international affairs. Both countries also have their own versions of exceptionalism; while the US believes in its manifest destiny, China also sees itself as an old civilisation that has won its right to primacy in world affairs. These two versions of exceptionalism obviously cannot co-exist without tensions. Moreover, mutual distrust is growing, strengthened by the fact that the two countries have very different political and economic systems. Indeed, given the tensions surrounding maritime disputes, one cannot rule out incidents at sea between US and Chinese naval ships, which could flare up into minor clashes. The competition for resources, markets and influence in Africa, Latin America and other parts of the world will also continue. Thus, one sees the beginnings of the classic Power Transition Theory being played out in Asia.

However, unlike the relations between the US and the erstwhile Soviet Union, relations between Washington and Beijing have different characteristics as the US and China are interdependent economically. Also, unlike the USSR and the US, there are substantial people-to-people links between the US and China. The US and China are also, as Secretary of State Hillary Clinton says, 'inescapably interdependent' today. The economic fortunes of the two countries are inextricably linked for the foreseeable future. While the US needs cheap Chinese products, China needs the American market and investments.

Despite its disagreements with the US, in the future too China will have to buy US treasury bonds for lack of attractive non-dollar currency alternatives, including the Euro. The US needs China to keep buying its treasury bonds because if China shifts out of its dollar assets, United States' long-term interest rates would go up and the price of US securities and value of the dollar would decrease, ultimately affecting the US economy and consumers adversely.

Thus, at least economically, the US and China have reached a state of Mutually Assured Survival. This, in turn, means that whatever the level of provocation from either side, the two countries have no option but to remain engaged and sort out issues before they escalate into major conflicts. Moreover, despite their differences on many issues in Asia, the two countries do cooperate on major global issues like terrorism, Afghanistan and climate change.

For the foreseeable future, it appears that the strategies of hedging and engagement will continue to direct relations between Washington and Beijing and the present scenario of 'cold peace' or uneasy co-existence will continue, ensuring USA's deepening and enduring role in the shaping of the Asian Century.

The United States in Southeast Asia

K. Yhome

Introduction

In November 2011, President Barack Obama attended the sixth East Asia Summit in Bali, Indonesia, the first time for a US president. The formal joining of the United States in the EAS has been described as 'a significant shift in American policy',[1] aimed at protecting its long-term strategic interests in Asia. In fact, Secretary of State Hillary Clinton published a feature article in the November 2011 issue of *Foreign Policy* magazine titled 'America's Pacific Century,' which stated clearly the US policy interests and direction.[2] Obama's participation also underscored the importance that Washington attaches to ASEAN and reaffirmed America's willingness to play a greater role in the rapidly changing economic and security landscape of the Asia-Pacific region.

In the past few years, during George W. Bush's presidency, many leaders in Southeast Asia had shown concern over a 'distracted' US. There was a view in Southeast Asia that the US interest in the region was on the decline as Washington focussed its attention on issues in the Middle East, Afghanistan and North Korea.[3] In the backdrop of the existence of such a notion, the Obama administration's re-engagement with the region has sent a strong signal of reassurance to the leaders of ASEAN.

This paper examines American strategic imperatives in Southeast Asia and attempts to understand the United States' evolving strategy in the new 'regional realities'. The primary factor driving the current US-Southeast Asia strategy is China's growing diplomatic, strategic and economic influence in the region. This paper argues that as Washington searches for viable strategic partners in Asia in the context of the fast-changing geostrategic environment, ASEAN has emerged as the keystone in America's long-term Asia strategy. Washington's strategy in Southeast Asia will continue to be driven by its geostrategic interests over the course of the coming decades, and it would be focussed on how the US can remain a major player by enhancing its economic and military presence in the region with the aim of influencing and shaping the evolving regional architecture in the context of the emerging power, China, challenging its pre-eminent position.

As the centre of gravity shifts to Asia, the geostrategic importance of Southeast Asia to the US has also increased.[4] The strategic importance of the region – both maritime and inland-mainland Southeast Asia – has emerged as a priority for the US in the context of growing regional tensions over maritime boundaries and competition for political, economic and strategic influence among major powers. These tensions have the potential of triggering regional instability that could adversely affect America's global strategic interests, and the evolving US strategy in Southeast Asia would aim at meeting these emerging challenges.

In the first section of this paper we examine the current US policy towards Southeast Asia by assessing recent trends in the relationship and in the second section we deal with the strategic drivers of the United States' Southeast Asia policy. It concludes with a perspective on future direction of US strategy in Southeast Asia and US-ASEAN relationship.

Recent Trends in US-Southeast Asia Relations

Since taking office in 2009, the Obama administration was quick to correct the notion that the US interest in the region was on the decline, by undertaking several initiatives to re-engage Southeast Asia, both at the bilateral and multilateral levels. Secretary of State Hillary Clinton visited Indonesia and the ASEAN Secretariat in February 2009 on her first official trip overseas and declared that the new administration under President Obama sought close relations with ASEAN. In July 2009, Clinton participated in the ASEAN Regional Forum (ARF) where she announced 'We're back' and subsequently signed the Treaty of Amity and Cooperation with ASEAN. In November 2009, President Obama and the leaders of all ASEAN members (including Myanmar) held their first ever summit meeting in Singapore and that was followed by another gathering in New York in September 2010. The US became a member of the EAS in October 2010 and participated in the first ASEAN Defence Ministers Meeting-Plus (ADMM-Plus). The US also appointed a special representative for ASEAN affairs. These initiatives conveyed a strong message of American commitment to remain in the region, and will go a long way in reshaping the nature of Washington's relations with Southeast Asia and in maintaining the United States' pre-eminent position in the Asia-Pacific region.

Defence Cooperation

Washington has also stepped up its military ties with Southeast Asian countries through a series of joint exercises and new defence agreements in the past couple of years. Some analysts think that the United States' increased military ties with Southeast Asia pose risks of a clash with China like the US-USSR confrontation of the Cold War.[5] In 2005, Washington normalised its relations with Vietnam and has sought to deepen its ties with that country. Their military-to-military ties have improved steadily since their restoration in 2003. In 2010 Vietnamese shipyards repaired two ships of the US Military Sealift Command (MSC). In August 2010, the United States and Vietnam conducted a week-long series of bilateral exercises that focussed on damage control and search and rescue operations, held aboard the *USS John S. McCain*. Furthermore, a delegation of the Vietnamese military and political officials was hosted aboard the carrier *USS George Washington* in the South China Sea. These moves on the part of the US indicate strengthening military ties with its old adversary and building trust between the armed forces of the two countries.

The exercises were followed by the first high-level defence dialogue between Washington and Hanoi that focussed on military exchanges, training and collaboration in search and rescue and humanitarian and disaster-relief operations, though Vietnam still remains banned under US legislation from receiving military equipment such as small arms, fighter aircraft or combat vessels. Vietnam has also recently shown signs of being receptive to US military presence in the region to counterbalance China and see it as a force that could provide the support for its claims in the South China Sea. Vietnam and the US have also signed a memorandum of understanding on civilian nuclear energy cooperation.

In June 2010, President Obama and Indonesian President Susilo Bambang Yudhoyono announced in Jakarta that the two countries would form a comprehensive strategic partnership. The agreement was intended to further integrate existing defence collaboration. A new defence cooperation agreement covers training, defence industry collaboration, procurement of military equipment, security dialogue and maritime security. In July 2010, the US also announced that it would resume cooperation with Indonesian Special Forces, though no immediate offer of the US-led training was made.[6] The agreement, however, removed the last obstacle to resuming full military relations between the two countries.

The events of 9/11 and the Bali bombings in 2002 gave new impetus to American efforts to improve relations with the world's most populous Muslim nation, and military relations have since steadily improved. In 2003, despite strong opposition from the Congress, funds were released for training Indonesian officers. This was followed in 2005 by the repeal of an arms embargo. Between 2006 and 2009, the US Global Train and Equipment Programme provided Indonesia with over $47 million to fight smuggling, piracy and trafficking. The installation of radar systems, particularly in the Makassar and Malacca straits, was also sponsored by the US Department of defence . In 2009, the US and Indonesia co-hosted the Garuda Shield multilateral military exercises in Bandung in which nine countries participated in drills focussed on peace support operations. In June 2010, another multilateral exercise was held in West Java to boost cooperation and professionalism in UN peacekeeping operations. Jointly organised by Indonesian and American militaries, soldiers from Thailand, the Philippines, Bangladesh, Nepal and Brunei took part. Indonesian troops also take part in the annual Cobra Gold exercises in Thailand.

The US has also initiated military ties with Cambodia. In July 2010, US and Cambodia co-hosted the 'Angkor Sentinel 10' multilateral military exercises with 23 countries. Although aimed at providing training in peacekeeping operations, these first exercises between the two countries are seen as a way for the US to get closer to Cambodia's military. The US has provided Cambodia with over $4.5 million in military equipment and training since 2006, and Cambodia joined the Cooperation Afloat Readiness and Training (CARAT) regional naval exercises for the first time in 2010.

The United States' interests in improving defence ties with Vietnam, Indonesia, and Cambodia are seen as a vital component of Washington's new strategy to re-engage Southeast Asia and to re-assert its commitment to the region's security. This re-engagement has often been viewed as aimed at countering China's growing assertiveness in territorial disputes and naval presence in the region, concerns shared by several ASEAN members. Both Vietnam and Indonesia occupy strategically important geographical positions in the South China Sea and the straits of Malacca and Makassar. They share a historical wariness of Chinese ambitions, a factor that is making them more willing to partner with the US.[7]

Economic Cooperation

After four years of negotiations, the United States concluded a trade and investment pact with ASEAN in August 2006, in an effort to strengthen its influence in the region which has been growing closer to China. The Trade and Investment Framework Arrangement

(TIFA) has been seen as a step towards a comprehensive free-trade agreement (FTA). ASEAN sees the TIFA deal as a recognition by Washington of the importance of ASEAN and as evidence of America's resolve to maintain its influence in the region. Through the TIFA cooperation framework, the US entered into Trans-Pacific Partnership (TPP)[8] negotiations that aim to create a free trade zone across the Pacific basin. Four Southeast Asian countries – Brunei, Malaysia, Singapore, and Vietnam – are already TPP-negotiating partners. The seventh round of the TPP talks was held in Ho Chi Minh City in June 2011.[9] The United States believes that Asia's integration into the global economy would benefit it and to this end, at the APEC summit in November 2011, President Obama focussed on trade and economic negotiations on the TPP with the aim to strengthen trans-Pacific linkages. During the meeting, a broad framework on the TTP trade agreement was announced.

Myanmar

The recent important developments in Washington's bilateral relations with individual Southeast Asian countries also provide an understanding of the evolving US strategy towards the region. One major irritant in the US-ASEAN relationship had been Myanmar, on which the US had imposed heavy sanctions over its lack of democratic reforms. In recent years, however, Washington has strongly demonstrated that it would not sacrifice its relationship with ASEAN over the issue. In fact, the United States has been narrowing the gap on regional issues with ASEAN. Washington reviewed its policy towards Myanmar in 2009 by combining engagement with existing sanctions. Strategic and security factors also seemed to have played a role in the US re-assessing its policy towards Myanmar. Among the Southeast Asian countries, China has the strongest ties with Myanmar and the US has been wary of

China-Myanmar strategic engagement. Washington has also shown concern over military ties between Pyongyang and Naypyidaw. The year 2012 witnessed rapid improvement in US-Myanmar relations evidenced by Secretary of State Hillary Clinton's visit to the country, followed by partial removal of sanctions, and the appointment of Derek Mitchell as US ambassador to Myanmar. Towards the end of 2012 there was some further relaxation of sanctions.

The Mekong Region

The US has been engaging the Mekong region through the Lower Mekong Initiative (LMI), a multinational effort between the US, Cambodia, Laos, Thailand and Vietnam aimed at 'foster[ing] integrated sub-regional cooperation' and capacity building in the areas of education, health, environment, and infrastructure where the US wants to 'make a positive contribution towards averting an environmental and socio-economic disaster' by offering assistance in technology, capacity-building and in assessment of environmental and socio-economic impacts. By initiating the LMI, the US is establishing an institutional entry into mainland Southeast Asia, which China considers its backyard. Disaster prevention and relief is seen as an area where the US could boost its image in the region.[10]

Even as the Obama administration has identified ASEAN as the keystone in its strategy in Asia, its recent initiatives are not without challenges. There have been voices of protest against Washington's military engagement with countries such as Cambodia. Human rights activists have protested against the inclusion of Cambodian military units linked to human rights violations in US military training programs.

US Strategic Imperatives in Southeast Asia

Southeast Asia is geo-strategically located at the crossroads of Asian powers – China, Japan and India, and is a critical part of the Asia-Pacific region. The region has a total population of 600 million and hosts the world's largest Muslim population – Indonesia alone is home to more Muslims than the entire Middle East. ASEAN's regional economy is over $1 trillion and it hosts the world's most strategic waterways through which pass 50 percent of global trade and one-third of the world's oil supplies. In the context of Southeast Asia's geostrategic importance to the overall stability of the Asia-Pacific region and US economy, the factors that drive US policy towards Southeast Asia include regional stability, counter-terrorism, business and access to the 'global commons' for the freedom of navigation.[11]

China has been able to increase its presence in Southeast Asia and deepen its ties with most of the Southeast Asia capitals in the past decade. A recent instance shows how China's influence in some of the countries in Southeast Asia has been used to favor its interests. In December 2009, the Cambodian government was pressured to deport 20 ethnic Uighurs – who Beijing claimed took part in the ethnic riots in Xinjiang province in July 2009. According to a commenter, 'The deportation of the Uighurs... showed that China's latent economic influence could be leveraged into considerable hard-power clout'.[12] While many Southeast Asian countries are concerned about China's rise, 'They [ASEAN countries] have no desire to choose between the United States – the region's de facto security guarantor – and China – a major driver of the region's economic prosperity'.[13]

Economic Interests

ASEAN has the fourth-largest economy in Asia, after China, India and Japan. As a developing region, its per capita income is low but its GDP is rapidly growing: an almost 170 percent increase over the past decade. ASEAN accounts for six percent of all world trade. The FTA negotiations between the US and ASEAN began in 2010 with six ASEAN members. China, India, Australia, New Zealand and South Korea have already finalised FTAs with ASEAN and are sharpening a competitive edge over the US in Southeast Asia. US-Southeast Asia trade amounted to over $176 billion in 2010. The US is ASEAN's third largest export market while ASEAN is the US' fourth largest export market.[14] US investments in ASEAN totalled $130 billion. Investment from ASEAN into the United States ranks fourth among Asian sources, totalling $11 billion.

Analysts feel that the US needs to get 'its game right' in the economic field. This view has also been expressed by a senior US senator calling for a FTA between the US and ASEAN. 'The United States should proceed to develop a comprehensive strategy toward engaging ASEAN in serious FTA discussions,' US Senator Richard G. Lugar, the Republican Leader of the Senate Foreign Relations Committee said in a statement.[15] He added that the United States' extensive trade restrictions on Myanmar 'should not deter US efforts to reach an FTA with the rest of ASEAN.' Senator Lugar also said that the Obama administration needs to 'announce a comprehensive and long-term strategy toward engaging ASEAN in FTA discussions... [and that the lack of a strong] signal [of] its commitment to developing a strategy for pursuing an FTA with ASEAN suggests to ASEAN leaders that they should first look to China, India and elsewhere for comprehensive trade interaction.

US actions are not matching US words of interest in expanding our relationship with Southeast Asia.'[16] Southeast Asians want the US and Japan to increase their business investment and official development assistance (ODA) in the region.

On the other hand, in the past decade or so, China's 'comprehensive diplomatic and economic campaign to court its southern neighbours' has 'transformed itself from a perceived threat into a partner'.[17] During the long US military engagement in Iraq and Afghanistan, China's economic ties with ASEAN countries have made phenomenal growth. As with other advanced economies such as Japan and the EU, China's trade with ASEAN overtook the US-ASEAN trade. China is today the biggest trade partner and the first export destination for ASEAN. Southeast Asian countries have also become a major source of investment for China. China's direct investment in ASEAN has reached $2.57 billion since the China-ASEAN FTA came into force in January 2010. In 2010, direct investment from ASEAN countries in China reached $6.32 billion, an increase of 35.2 percent. In 2010, trade volume between China and the ASEAN countries reached $292.8 billion, an increase of 37.5 percent year on year. The implementation of the China-ASEAN free trade area agreement is seen as an important mechanism in pushing forward the regional integration process of East Asia.[18] China's rise as a major regional power has posed a major challenge for the United States and the China-ASEAN FTA has further underscored concern that the United States is losing out to China in Southeast Asia. Washington's increasing focus on the region will, perhaps, alleviate these concerns.

Maritime Security

The South China Sea, one of the busiest shipping lanes in the world, has been the focal point of sovereignty disputes among its adjacent countries, namely China, the Philippines, Brunei, Singapore, Vietnam, Taiwan and Malaysia with the potential of becoming the flashpoint for US-China rivalry with geopolitical implications.[19] Some believe that Southeast Asia could become the ground where access to the global commons will be tested because of the critical position it occupies with vital sea lanes of communication (SLOCs) running through the region.

Until recently, the US appeared to have viewed China's desire for regional and global influence commensurate with its rising power as normal and to be expected, and that it need not necessarily conflict with US interests.[20] However, that seems to be changing in recent years primarily because of two major reasons. First, because of the increase in China's provocative behavior with regard to the maritime boundary issues in the South China Sea with its neighbours; and second, because of China's 'increasing assertiveness in pursuing its geopolitical interests'. Apart from China's aggressive behaviour towards its neighbours on the South China Sea disputes, the US has shown concern over China's pressure on US multinational companies to stop drilling in blocks offered by Vietnam and the harassment of US Navy ships in the South China Sea. In March 2009, the US Navy ship *Impeccable* was harassed in waters south of Hainan Island, and in June the same year a Chinese submarine collided with an underwater sonar array that the destroyer *USS John S. McCain* was towing. The US sees these incidents as 'concerted efforts to change the established rules to China's advantage'.

China's activities in Southeast Asia have been, directly or indirectly, affecting US strategic interests in the region. A clear change of the US position on the South China Sea disputes in the recent years suggests that Washington is willing to play a greater role in the region. Even as the US has called for the peaceful resolution of maritime territorial disputes and for non-interference in the rights of free passage of warships in the straits and exclusive economic zones, it did not take a stand on the issue when the Spratly incident took place in 1995. In July 2010, Secretary Clinton called for free passage in the disputed South China Sea and declared it as America's 'national interest'. Some see the South China Sea as a 'perfect stepping stone' for the US in its efforts to re-engage Asia. It has been argued that China's 'increasing muscle flexing over its maritime territorial disputes with Southeast Asian countries poses a growing problem for legitimate American and Southeast Asian interests, including freedom of navigation, access to rich undersea oil and gas deposits, and the cooperative and sustainable development of other seabed resources, fisheries, and estuaries. The consequences of China's behaviour in the South China Sea in particular include threats to regional peace and stability, economic development, traditional subsistence livelihoods, and food security'.[21] Washington's new stance on the South China Sea, however, is seen by some as 'not only the internationalisation of the South China Sea disputes, but also the opening of a potential new front in US-China rivalry'.[22]

As China undertakes major expansion of its military power, particularly its Navy, the implications on regional stability have caused concern to the US. China has been strengthening its power projection capabilities in the South China Sea by constructing a large naval base at Sanya in the Hainan Island, allowing its surface vessels and attack submarines to project power. The activities of the People's Liberation Army (PLA) Navy in recent years have demonstrated China's willingness to flex its muscles to support its territorial claims in South China Sea. The US views these incidents as aggressive signals on the part of China to demonstrate its 'dominance and control over the South China Sea'. The US assessment has been that China's intentions are not to fight the US directly, but US allies, such as Japan and the Philippines, are becoming vulnerable to China's growing military capabilities and Beijing may 'deny' the US 'the ability to come to the aid and defence' of its regional allies in the event of a conflict.[23]

Even as the US and South Korea have been conducting naval exercises in the Sea of Japan, China too has been carrying out military exercises in the South China Sea. Reasserting its strategic interests in the region, for instance, on 18 August 2010, the US commander of the Pacific Command, Admiral Robert Willard, reportedly said that Chinese assertiveness in the South China Sea was causing concern in the region but the US would work to ensure security and protect important trade lanes. South China Sea disputes have emerged as the most critical development in the maritime security and regional stability question in Southeast Asia. As Washington renews its engagement with Southeast Asia, China has been entangled in disputes with several neighbours in the region.

Regional Architecture

Another important strategic interest in Southeast Asia is the evolving Asian security and economic architecture. The US is increasingly recognising ASEAN's role in regional architecture. With Southeast Asia likely to remain the 'focal point' where the most important 'geostrategic game' will be played out in the next several years, the US sees ASEAN as a growing regional and global player.[24] The US and ASEAN also share common interests in strengthening regional institutions as a strategy to engage China. The US hopes that its continued engagement with the region will enable it to play a critical role in defining future Asian regional architecture. The US supports the aim of Southeast Asian nations to promote ASEAN's centrality in the region's security architecture. This actually is in the US' own interest also and, to this end, Washington is expected to put 'more diplomatic effort into consulting and coordinating with regional states in advance of ASEAN-related summits and ministerial meetings.'[25]

Promotion of Liberal Democracy

It is also one of the United States' long-term aims to promote liberal-democratic systems in Southeast Asia. Most mainland Southeast Asian countries have been going through political transitions accompanied by some instability. Human Rights issues will continue to emerge as irritants in US-ASEAN relations, and there have been voices of protest against military-to-military relations with some Southeast Asian countries. Most governments in Southeast Asia have weak democratic institutions, lack political accountability and have poor governance. The US believes moderate politics, democracy, international economic integration, effective governance and political accountability would favour its interests in the long-run and, therefore it wants to strengthen these areas. The US-Indonesia Comprehensive Partnership is seen as an important tool for realising USA's national interests in Southeast Asia and the Muslim world.

Non-traditional Security Issues

Several non-traditional security issues facing Southeast Asia are also of interest and concern to the United States. Washington needs the cooperation of Southeast Asian countries to tackle issues like radicalization of society and countering the growth of communist ideology, terrorism, etc. Another major concern of Washington is in the area of nuclear proliferation in the region. In this context Myanmar's ties with North Korea were viewed with suspicion though no credible evidence of Myanmar acquiring nuclear technologies from Pyongyang have so far been established. Secretary of State Hillary Clinton had expressed concerns over Myanmar-North Korea military ties during the ASEAN Summit in 2009.

The deepening Chinese involvement in infrastructure projects and hydropower dams on the rivers common to China and Southeast Asian countries are creating anxiety among the latter. This is another factor drawing the United States back into the region again after years of Washington's somewhat detached stance. The renewed US interest is welcomed by these countries as a clear response to their concern over potential instability due to China's assertiveness in the Mekong Basin and the South China Sea. The Obama administration has taken some 'positive steps' such as the LMI, which has been welcomed by the Mekong countries.

Conclusion

From the geostrategic perspective and in light of its own interests, the US sees Southeast Asia as a sort of 'fulcrum' for its long-term engagement in Asia. The region with critically important geographic location between the Pacific and the Indian Oceans is bound to have a major role in the structuring of Asian peace, stability, and power equilibrium. The emerging strategic dynamic, particularly China's growing assertiveness and increasing tension in the South China Sea, will strengthen the ties between the US and Southeast Asian countries despite differences on issues of democracy and human rights, and long-term US presence and proactive role in this part of Asia. This does not mean that relations between the US and China will necessarily be adversarial and confrontational.

While, not unlike the countries of the region, Washington is wary of China's strategic intentions, it also realises the need to work with China to tackle common challenges, including nuclear non-proliferation, terrorism, climate change and global economic stability. The ASEAN, while looking to the US for support in their relations with their powerful neighbour, also want to see good relations between Beijing and Washington so that they are not driven to choosing between the two.

Nevertheless, the US bilateral alliance architecture is an important reality in Asia's emerging regional architecture and even as the US tries to enhance its role in regional multilateral forums, sponsored or favoured by China, it will continue to strengthen its alliances and strategic partnership with Indonesia and Vietnam and with Singapore, Thailand and the Philippines.

Thus ASEAN will play a major role in keeping the US in Asia in the foreseeable future. At the tenth annual International Institute for Strategic Studies (IISS) Shangri-La Dialogue in Singapore in June 2011, US defence Secretary Robert Gates had said that the US will increase its military involvement in and commitment to Asia, especially Southeast Asia. Gates laid out several ways in which the US will step up its military presence in the region, adding attention and resources to military relationships with countries such as Singapore and Australia, in order to maintain America's position as the guarantor of regional peace and security.

The United States and South Asia

C. Raja Mohan

The Bush Legacy

The Obama administration might have returned the United States to East Asia, but it was George W. Bush who brought America back into South Asia at the turn of the millennium. Obama sought to build and improvise upon the Bush legacy in the South Asian subcontinent. The Bush administration had come to power in January 2001, determined to deal with the rise of China and organise a new great power balance that it said must 'favour freedom'. India, the world's largest democracy, had a special place in Bush's worldview. Bush decreed that Washington will assist India in its rise to great power status. The events of 9/11 had brought the United States, with a big bang literally, into the subcontinent. The focus on the war on terror in Afghanistan and Pakistan and its decision to invade Iraq and promote the democracy agenda in the Middle East inevitably detracted from Bush's initial emphasis on East Asia. At the end of eight Bush years, the rapid rise of China and the emergence of India had generated new linkages between South Asia and East Asia.

The United States had largely turned its back on South Asia after compelling the Soviet Union to withdraw from Afghanistan at the end of the 1980s. The consequences of the strategy adopted to achieve this goal, the promotion of jihad against god-less communists, came back to haunt the United States in the form of the al-Qaeda and many other organisations committed to violent religious extremism. Although the war on terror and stabilisation of Afghanistan saw a renewed American dependence on Pakistan, the US did not abandon the goal it had set for itself on transforming the relationship with India. Unlike in the 1950s and the 1980s, when larger strategic imperatives at the global level compelled the United States to privilege the relationship with Pakistan over that with India, the Bush administration sought to deepen the relationship with Islamabad and New Delhi simultaneously. Through a strategy that was called 'de-hyphenation', Washington focussed on building its relationship with the Subcontinental rivals, each on their own merit and avoiding a zero sum game.[1]

The US declared Pakistan a major non-NATO (North Atlantic Treaty Organization) ally and showered on it massive economic and military assistance in return for its support in the war on terror. India, in turn, was seen as a potential partner in building a stable Asian balance of power. For the first time, then, Washington's policies towards Pakistan and India were driven by two very different objectives. As part of its effort to overcome political distrust in New Delhi accumulated over the years, Washington addressed two important traditional grievances of India – a perceived American-tilt toward Pakistan in the dispute over Jammu & Kashmir and the prolonged blockade of high-technology flows in the name of defending the global nuclear order. On the former, Washington ended its traditional diplomatic activism to promote a solution, and on the latter actively promoted reconciliation between India and the international non-proliferation regime through the controversial civil nuclear initiative.

The Bush years also saw significant expansion of the India-US defence cooperation. While the policy of de-hyphenation succeeded, Washington had to occasionally intervene to defuse military/nuclear crises between India and Pakistan, and encourage them to embark on a dialogue to resolve bilateral issues. Whatever its effectiveness, the Bush administration pressed the Pakistan army to end its support to anti-India terror groups and stepped up counter-terror security cooperation with India. It was this legacy of simultaneous expansion of US engagement with India and Pakistan that Obama inherited from Bush. This legacy involved an interesting paradox. Although the war on terror and the preoccupation with Southwest Asia and the Middle East distracted American attention from dealing with the rise of China, the Bush administration's significant political investment in building a strategic partnership with India seemed to provide new options for America's Asian grand strategy.

This essay will focus on the two basic dimensions of US policy towards the subcontinent. One is the evolution of Obama's policy on the Af-Pak-India issues. The other is about Obama's attempts to balance the US engagement with China and India. The essay concludes with a brief discussion on the emerging geopolitical conception of the 'Indo-Pacific' in the Obama administration that breaks down the traditional divide between East and South Asia in the conceptualisation and execution of US policy.

The Af-Pak-India conundrum

Obama came to power criticising Bush for pursuing a 'war of choice' in Iraq while neglecting the 'war of necessity' in Afghanistan. Part of Obama's motivation was tactical, to outflank the predictable Republican criticism that the Democrats are weak on defence. Yet it is possible to argue that Obama recognised the strategic importance of bringing the war on terror to an early closure in Afghanistan. Even as he ordered a surge in US troop levels in Afghanistan, Obama was quite clear that the United States cannot fight this war for ever. Obama was also determined to recast relations with Pakistan by promising more aid while making Islamabad more accountable in the war on terror. Obama's advisers also believed that the Pakistan army will be more responsive to the US needs in Afghanistan if its concerns about India were met.[2] During his campaign and in the few weeks between election and assumption of office, Obama mused about appointing a special envoy to resolve the Kashmir question and his conviction that resolving Pakistan's problems on its eastern frontiers will help solve the US problems on its western frontier.[3]

In Delhi there was deep concern and resentment about the direction of Obama's Kashmir pronouncements. India was apprehensive that Obama was about to discard the Bush policy of de-hyphenation and return to the traditional Democratic approach of viewing India through the prism of Pakistan. Mounting a spirited campaign with the incoming administration, India managed to stop Obama from including India in the mandate of the special representative for Afghanistan and Pakistan that he announced within the first week of being sworn in. India remained mostly cool to Richard Holbrooke, who was appointed to this position, fearing that Kashmir and Indo-Pak issues were on Washington's agenda irrespective of the declared mandate of the special envoy. As he understood India's concerns, Obama avoided injecting himself into the Kashmir dispute, despite much pressure from sections of his administration.

While he did continue to speak about the importance of Indo-Pak reconciliation in a general way, he recognised the importance of avoiding the Kashmir minefield. Obama also stepped up counter-terror cooperation with India after the attacks on Mumbai at the end of November 2008. He also pressed the Pakistan army to shut down the camps on its soil of international terror outfits like the Lashkar-e-Tayyeba and bring the plotters of the Mumbai attacks to justice. This did not have much of an impact on Pakistan. As Obama came to terms with the fact that the Pakistan army was playing both sides of the street in the war on terror, he stepped up pressure on Rawalpindi by expanding drone strikes on the terror sanctuaries in the tribal borderlands of Pakistan. Obama also authorised increased Special Forces operations across the Durand Line into Pakistan. The new tensions between the United States and Pakistan boiled over when Obama ordered a raid on Osama bin Laden's hideout in the garrison town of Abbottabad without the permission of Islamabad. Rather than express contrition, the Pakistan army defined the issue as a violation of its sovereignty and retaliated by ordering US military and Central Intelligence Agency (CIA) personnel out of the country. The US in turn threatened to cut off military aid to Pakistan.[4]

If Obama's military strategy in Afghanistan complicated its ties with Pakistan, his plans to end US combat role in the country by 2014 and find a political reconciliation with sections of the Taliban created ripples across the Subcontinent and beyond.[5] While the US is negotiating the terms of a residual military presence with Kabul as part of a long-term strategic partnership agreement, the image of a US retreat from Afghanistan has gained ground. Delhi feared that the US would depart Afghanistan, leaving it at the mercy of Pakistan and the Taliban. In Pakistan there were worries about the US outreach to the Taliban independent of Rawalpindi. While the US wants Rawalpindi to destroy the Haqqani network, an ally of the al-Qaeda that enjoys sanctuary and state support in Pakistan, the army wants the group to be part of a final political settlement in Kabul. Seeking a definitive voice in the future political arrangements in Afghanistan, the Pakistan army has been negotiating directly with Kabul. Three weeks before the US raid on bin Laden, the prime minister of Pakistan, Yusuf Raza Gilani, and the Army Chief General Ashfaq Pervez Kayani travelled to Kabul and laid out their terms for settlement in Afghanistan. US media sources reported that Gilani and Kayani told Karzai that the US was a power in decline and that Kabul will have a greater chance of stability if it chose to align with China. It was re-alignment that the Pak army would be happy to facilitate.[6] The traditional debate in Asia had seen East Asian and Af-Pak theaters as two very different worlds. But the relative decline of the United States and rise of China, with its growing interests in Afghanistan and its long-term commitments to Pakistan, point to the futility of seeing these as separate worlds.

The Strategic Triangle

The subcontinent's role as the crossroads between eastern and western parts of Asia has been reinforced by the emergence of a 'strategic triangle' involving the United States, China and India in the Bush years. As in the Indo-Pak case, Obama had a bit of initial trouble managing the Bush legacy on China and India. There was little doubt in either Washington or Beijing that the

Bush administration's new warmth towards India was rooted in the perceived need to balance the rise of China in Asia. Although neither side wished to define their new partnership in terms of China's rise, Beijing was clearly the elephant in the room as Washington and Delhi sat across the table.[7] This clarity began to blur as Obama began to reframe America's Asia policy. Not everyone in Washington's foreign policy establishment believed in Bush's emphasis on building up India to structure a new Asian balance of power. As the Obama administration coped with the detritus of two wars, a massive financial crisis and deepening economic interdependence with China, confronting Beijing was out of question.

While everyone in Washington seemed to agree on the importance of re-engaging Asia at the dawn of the Obama administration, there were many who underlined the importance of building durable strategic cooperation with China. This line was reflected in the proposition that Washington and Beijing must build a new partnership, the so-called Group of Two, to manage the new international challenges from the financial crisis to global warming.[8] Although the administration itself did not use the term 'G-2', the concept gained currency as some pilloried it and others welcomed it. Delhi was firmly in the first camp and senior officials in the government publicly expressed concern about the potential consequences of a Sino-US condominium in Asia and beyond. India's concerns were magnified as Hillary Clinton, in her first trip abroad to Asia, skipped Delhi. As she traveled to Beijing, Clinton down-played concerns about human rights and underscored the importance of engaging China. The new approach of accommodating China reached its peak during Obama's visit to Beijing in November 2009, when the two sides declared their readiness to cooperate in promoting stability in South Asia.[9]

India reacted strongly against the American support to Chinese over-lordship over the subcontinent. India could not but recall the similarity with the Obama-Hu Jintao joint communique of November 2009, which was issued by President Bill Clinton and President Jiang Zemin in Beijing in June 1998, barely weeks after India's nuclear tests in May 1998. Unlike Clinton, Obama, however, had an opportunity to make quick amends as he hosted Prime Minister Manmohan Singh for the first state banquet at the White House in November 2009. Obama went out of the way to emphasise India's role as an Asian power.[10] While some skeptics saw this as little more than a formal reassurance, there was enough evidence to suggest that Obama was committed to build on the foundations laid down by Bush. Despite much reluctance in the administration, Obama pressed ahead with the implementation of the controversial civil nuclear initiative and expanded defence cooperation with India. A year later, he travelled to Delhi to endorse India's candidacy for permanent membership of the United Nations Security Council, agreed to support India's membership of the nuclear export control groupings and called for greater cooperation between India and the United States in the management of global commons—the oceans, outer space and cyber domains.[11] Visiting India a few months later, Clinton urged India to take on the leadership mantle in Asia and expressed strong support for a larger Indian role in Asia and the Pacific.[12] While some in India did not want to be seen as doing the US' bidding in Asia, Clinton's strategic enthusiasm certainly resonated with India's Asian aspirations that go back to the very founding of modern India.[13]

The new emphasis from Obama and Clinton on India's role in Asia marked a return to at least some of the assumptions of the Bush administration about Delhi's relevance to the organisation of a stable security order in Asia. This return was probably facilitated by the failure of Obama's outreach to China. Although Obama had offered some variant of G-2, the Chinese were not willing to accept the US terms for a rapprochement. Further, the Chinese assertiveness in Asia and its effort to undermine US alliances in Asia and constrict the US naval operations in the Western Pacific suggested China's ambitions were much larger than becoming a joint leader with the United States.

The years 2010-11 saw the United States and India launch new regional security dialogues on East, Central and West Asia. Washington and Delhi also agreed to initiate a triangular dialogue with Japan, which echoed the much criticised Bush initiative for a quadrilateral dialogue among the Asian democracies. While Obama seemed to move along the track developed in the Bush years, there have been fresh problems as well. There has been some disappointment in Washington at the failure of India to provide an effective liability regime for the participation of US companies in the building of nuclear power plants in India. Washington was also frustrated by the Indian decision to knock out Boeing and Lockheed from the competition for the purchase of the 126 fighter aircraft. The Pentagon too has been surprised by the Indian inhibition to promote interoperability between the two forces and the reluctance to undertake joint operations. In India, the Manmohan Singh government, which had undertaken so much political risk in building a new relationship with Washington, seemed to run out of steam in pushing the bilateral agenda. As the weakest of the three powers, New Delhi was also concerned that a weakening United States will be tempted to cut a deal with China rather than balance it. This in turn underlined for India the importance of repairing relations with China and maintaining an independent approach to Beijing.

Towards the Indo-Pacific

Despite its initial flip-flops towards South Asia and the many challenges it confronts in the region, the Obama administration has begun to engineer an important change in the American geopolitical conception about the region. On the one hand it has articulated the vision of Afghanistan's future as a bridge between the subcontinent and Central Asia. Hillary Clinton has called for greater flows of energy and commerce between the two regions as part of the effort to stabilise Afghanistan. 'An Afghanistan firmly embedded in the economic life of a thriving South and Central Asia would be able to attract new sources of foreign investment and connect to markets abroad, including hundreds of millions of potential new customers in India. And increasing trade across the region would open up new sources of raw material, energy, and agricultural products, creating more jobs in India, Pakistan, and Afghanistan'.[14] The potential implications of the rise of China and the partnership between Rawalpindi and Beijing has also underscored for Washington the meaning of China's rise, for Asia as a whole and not just East Asia. While the Obama administration has welcomed a larger Chinese role in stabilising Afghanistan, it cannot but begin to contemplate the consequences of Beijing's expanding influence in South and South-Western Asia in collaboration with Pakistan.

Equally significant is the repeated affirmation of the Obama administration on India's role in bridging the Indian and Pacific Oceans. As Clinton told her audience in Chennai, a port city facing Southeast Asia: 'The United States has always been a Pacific power because of our very great blessing of geography. And India straddling the waters from the Indian to the Pacific Ocean is, with us, a steward of these waterways. We are both deeply invested in shaping the future of the region that they connect.'[15]

Given simultaneous rise of China and India their intersection of interests across all of Asia, the strategic community in the United States has begun to recognise the importance of developing an integrated strategy towards East and South Asian regions. As China seeks to establish a presence in the Indian Ocean, India announces itself in the Western Pacific, and Asia's maritime disputes acquire a new edge, securing the Indo-Pacific commons has become an important element of the US strategy towards the region.[16] As the pre-eminent maritime power that has managed the order in the two oceans for the last many decades but facing new challenges from a rising China, the United States is now seeking a strong security partnership with India in the Indo-Pacific. As the American and Indian navies find that they have no option but to work together in the waters of the Indian and Pacific Oceans, the traditional differentiation between these two theatres is likely to rapidly disappear.

Is America Leaving Afghanistan?

Saeed Naqvi

In 1943, during a conversation with Lord Halifax, British ambassador to Washington, President Roosevelt was quite unambiguous about Anglo-American coordination in the Persian Gulf.

'Persian oil is yours; we share the oil of Iraq and Kuwait. As for Saudi Arabian oil, it's ours'.

When Lord Halifax returned from his posting in Washington in 1946, Lord Mountbatten was packing his bags to take up residence in New Delhi. Lord Halifax had earlier been foreign secretary too. It is unlikely that in-depth discussions were not held on British Indian policy towards the oil-rich Gulf.

From 1925 to 1934, Lord Halifax, in his incarnation as Lord Irwin, had also seen King Zahir Shah ascend the throne in Kabul where the British had abiding interest since the Great Game, thwarting Czarist Russia. By the time Mountbatten arrived in India, the new enemy was Soviet Russia. A full blown Cold War was in place.

A combination of two factors – Gulf oil and a menacing Soviet Union, spurred Anglo-American interest in the real estate that was to become Pakistan, particularly the North-Western part of the Indian subcontinent.

In his book, aptly titled, *The Shadow of the Great Game: The Untold Story of India's Partition*, Narendra Singh Sarila, former aide-de-camp (ADC) to Mountbatten, Indian ambassador to Switzerland and France has spelt out British interests with great clarity:

'The agreement to partition India was announced on 3 June 1947. The following week the British Labour Party's annual conference was held in Margate. There, addressing the delegates, Ernest Bevin, the British Foreign Secretary, stated that the division of India "would help to consolidate Britain in the Middle East".' On reading Bevin's remarks, Krishna Menon asked Mountbatten if the northwest of India 'abutting Afghanistan and Iran is still the hinterland of the imperial strategy?' Of course it was.

British interest in the Middle East (and therefore in Pakistan, Afghanistan and Iran) remained consistently focussed throughout the Cold War. This interest did not flag even after the Soviet Union's collapse. Asked by journalists in Finland, if Britian still needed her nuclear deterrent now that the Soviet threat was over, Mrs. Thatcher snapped back: 'We need our nuclear arsenal because there is still a problem in the Middle East'.

In the late 1970s, two countries of strategic interest, Afghanistan and Iran, slipped out of Western control. The Saur or the April Revolution in Afghanistan brought the two communist parties, Khalq and Parcham, to power; paving the way for Soviet arrival in Afghanistan in 1980. By this time, the Shah had calamitously been replaced by Ayatollah Khomeini in Teheran.

To meet the sudden loss of power in a region about which the West had thus far been quite sanguine, the James Carter administration set-up a Rapid Deployment Force to meet any further contingencies. But on a more permanent basis, the Pacific Command was split into Commander-in-Chief, Pacific Command (CINCPAC) and CENTCOM (Central Command).The latter, was to focus on the entire region from Pakistan right upto Aden.

To expel the Soviets from Afghanistan, the US, Saudi Arabia and Pakistan got into a scrum. The idea of producing an extreme, Salafist Islam was to serve three purposes. The US priority was to see the back of the Soviets from Afghanistan. The other two were also interested in this outcome but they had their own priorities, as well.

For Zia-ul-Haq, Arabised Islam would wrench Pakistan away from the cultural pull of Indian Islam, with its tolerance for music, arts, culture and respect for Hindu mythology and folklore. This, according to him, would help resolve Pakistan's existential issue of its identity, as something totally different from India.

The Saudis had twin interests: to have an entrenched, Saudi Salafism in Afghanistan as a bulwark against the Shiaism of the Ayatullhas in Iran. Also, since the Saudis were embarked on the manufacture of mujahideen in the Salafist mould, they set up another manufacturing unit in Yemen too where this variety of Muslims would help thwart Soviet influence in South Yemen, primarily Aden. This was the origin of the al-Qaeda in the Arabian Peninsula.

Never in history has a project gone so woefully wrong. It boomeranged on its authors. That was the genesis of the al-Qaeda, Taliban, indeed extremism wearing an Islamic cloak, which resulted in 9/11, entrenched Talibans in Afghanistan and promoted unbridled terrorism in Pakistan.

And now, with President Barack Obama in the White House for his second term, a great deal of the choreography centres around Afghanistan and Pakistan. With US-Pak relations plummeting into an abyss, Washington appears bereft of all options except to stay on in the neighbouring country, Afghanistan, to keep a watchful eye on the world's only Muslim nuclear-armed country teetering on the brink. For Pakistan-watching, there is no watch-tower better than Afghanistan. But there is a general incantation that the US has no stomach for continued armed intervention in Afghanistan. The Afghan war, we are being asked to believe, is unpopular. What is the gauge that measures the popularity or otherwise of a war? Opinion polls, we are told.

If the Afghan war is unpopular, it makes imminent sense for Obama to pull out to gain even more popularity at home. But if he pulls out – drawdown is the current term – from which real estate does the US keep a watch on the world's most dangerous place, Pakistan?

Since a realistic answer cannot be given to a question so posed, the Obama team has decided to do a Marcel Marceau Mime act in which a man appears to be running fast from Afghanistan but is actually standing still. All manner of stories are afoot. A limited number of combat troops will begin to leave Afghanistan.

Even as the all important NATO Summit in Chicago on 20-21 May 2012, focussed exclusively on Afghanistan, there was no clarity on how US military involvement was to be navigated.

For instance, until early 2011 President Barack Obama was committed to July 2011 as the date from when American troops would start to withdrawn from Afghanistan. And yet those whose job it was to supervise this withdrawal introduced caveats: that July 2011 is not cast in stone; withdrawals will be conditioned by the situation on the ground; only combat troops will be withdrawn; the Afghan National Army has to be ready to take over; and so on. Well, now we are being told that 3,200,000 Afghan troops are all but ready. What does 'all but' mean?

General Stanley McChrystal, the former commander of US and NATO troops, had openly stated that the popularity of India's socio-economic development work in Afghanistan creates complications and distracts Pakistan from its war-on-terror focus. His successor, Gen. David Petraeus did his bit to placate and humour Pakistan by talking privately of India's 'Cold Start' doctrine: A doctrine buried in India's military archives, one which is not part of any strategic discourse. But Islamabad was able to sell this lemon to Petraeus. This is frequently cited by Afghan policymakers as an example of Pakistan's 'apparent' centrality to US purposes in the region.

Obama remained true to the promise he made on 1 December 2009 at the United States Military Academy at West Point. He had said that in the first half of 2010, there would be an induction of 30,000 additional troops. Augmentation in troop strength promptly took place. But have the accomplishments of the surge been sufficient to guarantee withdrawal by a certain date?

Since it were the Taliban who accorded hospitality to the al-Qaeda, guilty of having sent 19 men in four aircraft to fly into targets in the US on 11 September 2001, there was severe US retaliation. The Taliban were ousted from Kabul in October 2001. It will remain a mystery why Saudi Arabia remains exempt from American ire, when 17 of the 19 who flew into the twin towers were from that country!

Then, the Bonn Conference convened by the UN Secretary General, set-up in President Obama's words recently, 'a provisional' government under President Hamid Karzai. But that 'provisional government' has lasted nine years. Indeed, at the 20 July 2010 Kabul Conference convened by the UN, Karzai almost established his indispensability by obtaining a mandate (from the conference) that he would continue as president until 2014. By that date, he said, the Afghan army and police would be ready to takeover from the US and the NATO forces. This, precisely, is what the US is saying today. Indeed, Karzai wants the Afghan presidential election advanced to 2013 so there is no cluttering of events when US withdrawal begins in 2014.

If President Karzai is to remain in Kabul till 2014, surely he will require protection till then and after. If the US and NATO are to start withdrawing in 2013, or 2014, given the caveats mentioned above, there will still be need for Karzai to be protected or accorded safe passage. Nobody has put up the case that by 2014 Karzai will capture the hearts and minds of all Afghans. We have some sort of script until 2014. But even this script could change.

Yes, the mounting death toll (4,000 coalition soldiers) and the costs of the war ($537.8 billion) against the backdrop of a declining western economy, are all good reasons for the US to leave Afghanistan. Supposing the death toll is brought down to, say, double digits annually and the costs of combat are substantially reduced, will the Americans still leave?

According to Russian estimates there are 30 US bases in Afghanistan. Of these, the ones at Bagram, Jalalabad, Kandahar, Helmand, Shindand (Herat), Mazar-e-Sharif are, by the sheer volume of masonry and architecture, not temporary. These bases will remain. Are we then talking about a qualified departure?

If the US is actually planning departure, why is it building a consulate in the heart of Mazar-e-Sharif on a scale which would dwarf large embassies? Renaissance is the only reasonable hotel in Mazar-e-Sharif. An entire section of which was, at one stage, transformed into a dormitory for the labour working on the US consulate. To the two gigantic blocks in the fortified embassy in Kabul with 700 personnel, a larger block is being added! US diplomats and army officers in large numbers are learning Pushto and Darri back in the US. Are these the looks of a power that is planning to leave Afghanistan?

If all these preparations for an extended non-combat stay in Afghanistan do, in some parlance or the other, tantamount to military departure, so be it. The US was supposed to have left Iraq. But 50,000 troops will remain in the various bases which are, ultimately, like country houses – open the locks and they are fully functional again.

I have seen the US, after bombing Serbia relentlessly for 72 days, create the independent state of Kosovo. But, while departing, they left behind the largest US base since the Vietnam War, Camp Bondsteel, abutting Macedonia. Also, an entire hill had been taken over in Skopje, capital of Macedonia, to build an embassy larger than a medium-sized Indian Fort. Guarding energy routes from the Black Sea or elsewhere is one of its obvious strategic interest in this area. Russians are probably doing much the same thing in Abkhazia and Ossetia.

These are the ways Great Powers function. It does not take them long to develop more than one focal point of interest once they have entered an area of strategic significance. It would therefore be wrong to imagine an America-free Afghanistan in the foreseeable future. Phasing out of some combat troops may happen. The bulk of it would probably retire to the six major bases – exuding power, but careful not to exert it, both internally and regionally. The 'invisibility' of US troops may remove the target of Afghan Taliban's anger. But there still remain concerns that these bases are crouched in a live, acrimonious theater. Moreover, the barrage of Drone attacks in both Afghanistan and Pakistan will keep local population in a sufficient state of agitation to warrant US-NATO presence.

Supply lines to these bases will have to be secured. This means control over Karachi port, and reports from Karachi are incrementally alarming. The recent political, ethnic and sectarian violence took a toll of 100 lives over three days. There is every sign that such incidents will increase. Burning of the Quran, killing of 26 Pakistani soldiers, urinating on dead Afghans, raping and killing of women and children – these horrendous acts will not be forgiven by Pashtuns on both sides of the border.

The rest of the route from Karachi through Balochistan to Afghanistan is never too far from the Taliban and the al-Qaeda friendly areas, whether in Quetta or in Kandahar. This leads to another major US requirement: the security of Pakistan, a country fighting on multiple fronts. At this crucial juncture, US-Pak relations have plummeted, perhaps irretrievably.

The supply route once gave Islamabad considerable leverage over the US. But to retain this leverage Pakistan must have control over strategic territory. This leads to finger-pointing at real or imaginary 'mischief' from India. Balochistan's border with Iran has occasionally livened up. What is not discussed sufficiently is the internal instability, in particular the insurgency in Balochistan.

What is beginning to worry Pakistan greatly is the effectiveness of the Central Asian supply route for US troops in Afghanistan. This dispensability of Pakistan could prove galling for Islamabad. If in panic the civilian government strikes a deal, which to the anti-American public appears degrading, it will lose the coming elections.

But alternative supply routes are expensive. Americans therefore have an abiding interest in Baloch and indeed, Pakistani stability. There is, of course, no dearth of theorists suggesting this route could be tactically used vis-a-vis the Gwadar port the Chinese have built. In other words there are multiple interests in the Baloch supply route.

What is making things extremely awkward for the US is that its quest for 'uncomplicated' coordination with Pakistan in controlling Afghan Taliban is hurtling headlong into complications.

Former Taliban ambassador to Pakistan Abdus Salaam Zaeef, 42, a follower and friend of Mullah Omar who spent four years in Guantanamo Bay, puts it bluntly: 'Pakistan simply has no role in Afghanistan'. This contradicts the apparent US line to the effect that Pakistan does indeed have a role in that country. After all, it was Pakistan's Inter Services Intelligence (ISI) which set up the mujahideen force in the 1980s, which has morphed into today's Taliban and the al-Qaeda.

But that was in another era. Today, such US rationalisations make Zaeef retort: 'Pakistan has proved to be unreliable. They provided the bases and every kind of help for the Americans to invade our country.' He feels that, 'The manner in which Pakistan has treated our prisoners is worse than Israeli treatment of Palestinian prisoners.' Zaeef adds, 'For four years I was at Guantanamo. Human rights violations were not as bad in Guantanamo as they are in Pakistan. For countless years our boys are languishing in Pakistani prisons without trial.' He goes on to suggest that, 'all this is talk. When Americans ask me about negotiations, I tell them to talk to those they are fighting – namely the Afghan Taliban.' The Pakistan army is fighting the Pakistan Taliban and 'those two can talk if they like,' but 'Pakistan has no business in Afghanistan.' All of this is said on TV. Well, this script did appear to have been adopted by the US when they started talking to Taliban in Qatar. The process has not gained much traction.

Zaeef believes talks with the Americans are possible, but insists on keeping Pakistan out. He has official armed protection around his house. 'Yes,' he says, when asked if he has spoken to Karzai and the US generals. Karzai corroborates, saying that he has been speaking to various 'Afghans', including Zaeef, to 'test the waters, as it were'.

I asked Zaeef if he knew anything about discussions with Sirajuddin Haqqani's group. 'These are rumours, not truth,' he said. Zaeef is unclear why Taliban attacked the Indian embassy. 'There are 64 intelligence agencies in Afghanistan and 47 countries with some troops in ISAF', he explains. 'You never know with certainty what is going on.'

Other Afghans working closely with to the intelligence agencies believe the Haqqani group was responsible for attacks on Indian interests. Why? Because that group, they claim, is under the ISI's control. Zaeef reacts with an emphatic denial. Pakistan, he says, has forfeited whatever control it had over groups in Afghanistan. 'For the Afghans, Pakistan is a trouble maker.'

On balance, what emerges is a Pakistani hand here and there without any overt approval or legitimacy accorded to it in Afghanistan at most levels. During my recent travels in Afghanistan, I was quite astonished at the dismal image Pakistan has in Afghanistan – in Pashtun and non-Pashtun areas alike.

Imagine a Pakistani group in a neighbouring Muslim country. You would think every member of the group would be dressed the Afghan way, in a Pathan suit or salwar-kameez. But the Pakistanis at the hotel where I stayed wore jeans or trousers and almost pretended to be Indians. The tall Pashtun gatekeeper asked me if I knew the other 'Indians' in the hotel. He was pointing to those Pakistanis who, by their bearing – deliberate or otherwise – came across as Indians to him. They never stepped out of the hotel. Astonishing though it may sound, it is uncomfortable to be a Pakistani in Afghan cities. Indians feel insecure only for one reason – Pakistan's ISI. Americans, President Karzai, Taliban sympathisers, security agencies, non-Pashtun leaders in Mazar-e-Sharif, Balkh, Bamyan – all are unanimous on this.

After talking to leaders, US officials, journalists, vice chancellors, governors, NGOs and film-makers across Afghanistan, I have come to this firm conclusion: The most unpopular government (not the people, as even Zaeef kept emphasising) in Afghanistan is the Pakistan government. The second on the hate list, after Pakistan, is Britain. Why? Partly, it is historical. Afghans have a long memory of the 'great game' and the Afghan wars. Also, the British had been very rough with 'natives' in Helmand during current operations.

The next on the 'mischief makers list' according to Afghans I met, is Iran. This image prevails more in the Pashtun areas because Iran played a key role in ousting the Taliban (Pashtuns) from Kabul in 2001. The fact of Iran being a neighbour accentuates its hovering presence. In North and West Afghanistan, the waxing and waning of the Persian Khorasani and Afghan civilisational overlap through millennia has left behind psychological bruises, with very thin scabs over them.

The attitude towards Americans is a paradox: anti-Americanism is there, but the passion of it is dissipating because other targets of collective dislike have emerged, Pakistan in the main. The Americans are omnipresent, but increasingly less 'palpable'. Also, the mushroom growth of 32 TV stations, 73 radio stations and over 500 daily and weekly publications has helped create a US-neutral audience. This is unlike Pakistan, where Musharraf unleashed a chaotic, unbridled media.

Almost by default, India has ended up having played a good hand not only by 'not making trouble', but also by being genuinely helpful. Building roads, hospitals, schools and providing training to Afghan civil servants, accepting students in Indian institutions, providing hospital facilities in Delhi – all of this has helped. But what beats it all is the immense popularity of Bollywood. At another cultural plane, the *rais* or the chief priest of Mazar-e-Sharif, Atiq Ullah Ansari, was eager to have the latest DVD collections of Bismillah Khan, Ali Akbar Khan and Ravi Shankar. I was amazed to meet people in Kabul who knew 'Saket', an upcoming South Delhi address. Why? Because of the row of hospitals there that Afghan patients have been patronising. When bids were invited years ago to construct the US-financed Kunar road near Peshawar – the Kunar river flows from Afghanistan to Peshawar – the best quotation reportedly came from Pakistan. But the project was given to an Indian company. While one must resist the temptation of reading too much into such decisions, their message should not be ignored either.

Former Algerian Foreign Minister and former UN envoy to Iraq and Afghanistan Lakhdar Brahimi says that the Taliban, particularly Afghan Taliban, do not trust Pakistan, specifically because the ISI have been manipulating them for decades. Brahimi also believes that Indians have traditionally had excellent relations with Pashtuns. Brahimi and former deputy secretary of state, Thomas Pickering, would therefore like India to sign in on negotiate-with-the-Taliban agenda. Though their diagnosis of India's historical links with the Pashtuns is correct (recall Rabindranath Tagore's *Kabuliwallah*), their prescription that India should side with the groups planning negotiations with Taliban would find New Delhi on the wrong side of one of these groups. One group was at the very heart of the Northern Alliance that fought the Taliban with the help of India, Iran and Russia, behind the leadership of a Che Guevera type romantic persona of the great Tajik leader, Ahmad Shah Masood.

The Brahimi school argues that the Taliban had roundly defeated the Northern Alliance and gained control over all of Afghanistan by 1996. That is not entirely true, because the CIA helped them. The power structure in Kabul that Karzai and NATO inherited on 22 December 2001 was largely Tajik with a sprinkling of Uzbeks and Hazaras. This became possible because of the Indian-Iranian-Russian-CIA coordination in 2001.

Every city square and official building in Afghan cities has a larger than life photograph of the charismatic Tajik leader, Ahmad Shah Masood. This is in memory of the Northern Alliance, of which Masood was the tallest leader, having ousted the Taliban from Kabul. These memorials have a symbolic significance. The Taliban, should they ever be part of the power structure in Kabul, will instantly remove them.

To restore ethnic balance, photographs of Ahmad Karzai have been mounted side by side the Masood photographs. But Karzai is not as tall a Pashtun as Masood was a Tajik – not by a long shot. Ask any Pashtun what he thinks of Masood's photographs in city squares and government buildings, and he shrugs his shoulders disapprovingly. The response of the non-Pashtun is one of reverence. This signifies a critical divide.

Afghanistan has gone through so much turmoil that Indian support to the Northern Alliance is a forgotten episode for the Pashtuns. Given this amnesia, the Indian profile has ready acceptance on all sides, a shining example of *diplomacy by default* – a slow tortoise-like movement which offends no one. More concretely, India's development activity and assistance, which directly benefits the people, attracts and pleases the Afghans.

The day when the ISI had a free run of the country, with the Saudis and the Americans in toe, is long gone. It is a brand new situation. India and the world need to look at this with clear eyes. President Hamid Karzai now has a glow of self-confidence on his face that was not there when I met him five years ago. One is restricted by the fact that the hour-long conversation with him is off the record. But let me give a gist of what Karzai's advisors say. 'The US is not fighting terror where it is nurtured'. This accusation at a US-Pak collusion cuts across all ethnic and regional groups in Afghanistan. In fact, Karzai wrote to Obama about Pak recalcitrance. Is he not talking to the Haqqani group? Karzai does not mind being quoted on his response: 'Haqqani is the worst of the lot!'

There are three issues on which Karzai is willing to be quoted:

1. The US is not striking at sanctuaries of terror in Pakistan. 'This helps Pakistan'.
2. India is not applying pressure on the US to do just that. 'This again helps Pakistan'.
3. Prime Minister Manmohan Singh should 'individually or collectively' sit down with the Pakistani leadership and have a 'heart to heart chat' so Islamabad does not go running to the Americans with stories of 'Indian plots'.

'I urge New Delhi to put pressure on the US to stop Pakistani mischief,' Karzai says. To Gen. Kayani, he says, 'Please don't do it, don't destabilise Afghanistan for your ends.' These are a few of the things he told me. Surprisingly, Karzai's narrative on US and Pakistan is not dissimilar to that of his political and ethnic detractors.

A sharp analyst of the current situation is the Tajik Amrullah Saleh, former head of the National Security Services in Afghanistan. According to his advisors: *Earlier, the US wanted to defeat the Taliban; now they want to weaken them. For his own reasons, perhaps, Karzai too does not wish to defeat them. The enemy is headquartered in Pakistan and he should be defeated there. For the US the 'expendable' part of the Taliban is in Afghanistan. Karzai asks why would he ever want to collaborate with NATO to kill the Afghans they consider expendable? (Emphasis added) (So says Saleh)*

Moreover, if Pakistan can survive playing a double game, why can't I? (asks Karzai).

There are three games going on:

1. The Taliban game is to expand and they are succeeding. The US and the new Afghan forces have been only controlling the Taliban. The government has no interest in fighting them. Karzai believes Taliban expansion is Pashtun expansion, which in the long run is in his interest.
2. The NATO has no strategy in the region because they have no policy towards Pakistan. They know they cannot defeat the Afghan Taliban without hitting hard at their bases in Pakistan. They are doing it belatedly but without Pak support. This is creating unspeakable anti-Americanism across the board in Pakistan.
3. The Saleh school of thought continues: 'They want to secure and build here. Instead of spending $90 billion here why don't they go and bomb the Rawalpindi GHQ? In 2005 you could travel to any part of Afghanistan safely. Today it is impossible to go anywhere – Taliban have spread all over. So, the US probably has a hidden agenda, because their transparent agenda is just not working. And they know it.'

Much of the current confusion is because Karzai has decided to become a dominant player. Part of his strategy is to say 'no' to Americans. Given the undercurrent of anti-Americanism, this thumbing of the nose at the Americans, he believes, expands his base. He will not consolidate his leadership if he keeps saying 'yes' to the US.

Therefore, it's 'no' to the American anti-corruption drive, foreign security companies, good government agenda, anti-Taliban agenda. 'No' to all this despite the presence of 110,000 US–NATO troops? The implication in Saleh's framework is clear. Is Karzai being allowed to strike this stance to grow into a durable leader? Because the United States' inability to restrain him is puzzling. And now that Karzai is showing his hand, it is along expected lines: he wants one of his clan to succeed him.

There are those who believe Karzai's anti-Americanism is a function of American 'helplessness' in the given situation. Either way, the moot point is: Who is gaining from this 'negotiate with the Taliban' talk – the Taliban or Karzai?

Vicious ethnic clashes broke out in West Kabul in August 2011 between Hazaras (shias) and Koochis, a nomadic sect of Pashtuns. Houses and shops were burnt and people killed. 'Where do you think will the Koochi Pashtuns turn for help?' asks Saleh. 'Towards Karzai or Taliban who are being projected as the future?' After a pause: 'Obviously towards Taliban.'

The Koochi–Hazara clash could well be the thin end of the wedge. Such Pashtun–non-Pashtun clashes could erupt all over Afghanistan, a sort of ethnic cleansing because Pashtun and Taliban will become increasingly interchangeable terms. The suggestion for talks with Taliban could well gain momentum, leading to a popular clamour among Pashtuns for power in Kabul. Power to the Pashtuns, or power to Taliban are just echoes of each other as far as the Pashtuns are concerned. 'There is only one issue on which some of us have doubts – treatment of women.' There is a whispering propaganda that this time Taliban will behave differently. Brahimi and Pickering are of this belief.

It is generally believed that there is some Taliban presence in most of the 34 Afghan provinces. South and East Afghanistan are considered overwhelmingly Pashtun territory. Robert Blackwill, a well-known security expert has proposed the partition of Afghanistan. In his framework, the US forces would maintain military control of the North and the West of Afghanistan. Pashtuns (or the Taliban), who form the majority in the South and East, would be allowed to govern this territory – this is unnecessarily placing on Washington the odium of a surgery which, in the given circumstances, may well emerge as part of an automatic evolutionary process.

Khan Abdul Ghaffar Khan, the renowned 'Frontier Gandhi' of the independence movement, had made a prediction on the 'idea of Pashtunistan'. Shortly before his death, he had collected his family at his village of Charsadda, near Peshawar, and made known his will: He should be buried in Jalalabad, East Afghanistan. The family fell into deep thought: Why was this great man making life difficult for them by wanting to be buried in another country? Ghaffar Khan told them: 'One day all these Pashtun areas, on both sides of the Durand line, will be one.'

As things stand, in the governance of South and East Afghanistan, Kabul has diminishing control. Likewise, in several tribal agencies of Pakistan's Pakhtoon-khwna, the former North West Frontier Province (NWFP), insurgencies are raging. When Rawalpindi general headquarters, egged on by the Americans, hits hard at the Taliban from the air, Pashtun nationalism flares up. When the GHQ softens, Taliban mops up the sympathies. It is a no-win situation. Overall, the control of Islamabad is negligible in Pashtun areas. And even though there are unbreakable ties of kinship between the two Pashtun populations living on both sides of the Durand line, social evolution in the two areas has been somewhat different.

Ever since Nur Mohammad Taraki took over as prime minister in 1978, the communist rule under his successors, Hafizullah Amin and Babrak Karmal, had weakened and altered old structures. Among Pashtuns there are two principal tribal streams – Durranis and Ghilzais. When President Mohammad Daud Khan was killed and Nur Mohammad Taraki took over as the communist prime minister, 200 years of Durrani rule ended. Taraki was a Ghilzai as is Mullah Omar. Karzai is a Populzai who come under the Durrani umbrella. This incipient tussle cannot be ignored. The Ghilzai, in power for 32 years, sees in Karzai a possible resurrection of the Durrani line. So, Karzai's dream of continuing the Populzai (Durrani) will never be accepted by the majority of Pashtuns or Taliban who are Ghilzais.

Soviet occupation brought to the fore younger commanders who undermined the power of the traditional village chief. That is another tussle. Then, the Civil War brought out a new cast of characters, at national, regional and local levels; it was a Pashtun and largely Tajik tussle. The rule of the Taliban upturned all previous structures until they were removed by the US and NATO, with the Northern Alliance in the vanguard. On the Pakistan side of the Af-Pak border, old structures have remained stable. It was this stability which enabled the Pakistan Taliban or Pashtuns to open their 'hujras' or hospitality quarters to the waves of Afghan Taliban or Pashtuns.

The more educated of the Afghan Pashtuns read the Pashtun categories in Pakistan with some precision. They divide the Pak Pashtuns into three categories:

1. First, there are Pashtun or Pathans who cocktail in Lahore. This is an influential segment, seduced by the Punjabi social

swing. The traditional anti-Punjab sentiment is subdued in this lot.

2. The nationalist Pashtuns resort to anti-Punjab rhetoric only when out of power, but are easily co-opted by the Central authority once in power. Asfandayar Wali (Frontier Gandhi's grandson) of the National Awami Party and their supporters would fall into this category.
3. The expanding category is the Islamist Pashtuns – the ones who were either reared in madrasas on the Pakistan side of the border or those having links with them. This is the ever increasing catchment area for recruitment of Taliban.

The first two categories are not separatists; they are opportunists. A Blackwill-like plan sets the cat among the pigeons in this lot. Equally, such a plan resonates well with the third category, barring those held on a tight leash by the ISI. At what stage will they be straining at the leash, even snapping at it? Bits and pieces of Afghan history, buried in amnesia, may well resurface in reaction to a reversal to Taliban rule or Pashtun consolidation. Afghanistan is a mosaic of different tribes and ethnicities: although anyone living within the geographical borders of Afghanistan is an Afghan. Amir Amanullah, greatly influenced by Turkey's Mustafa Kemal Atatürk, diligently went about knitting the Afghan state by transferring Pashtun populations to Tajik, Uzbek and Hazara-dominated areas of the country to avert any future disintegration on ethnic lines. Likewise, other ethnic populations were settled in Pashtun areas. Large parts of Afghanistan are a patchwork of ethnic minorities.

These islands of minorities could well become targets, should a Taliban or Pashtun entity begin to emerge. Conversely, should these 'islands' remain the way they have been, clashes with NGOs and ISAF personnel would warrant the presence of NATO and

US forces. In other words, there are local incentives, disincentives and options.

When I asked Mullah Zaeef what he thought of a 'regional conference' on Afghanistan to underwrite the nation's independence and territorial integrity, his response was categorical: 'Iran, Uzbekistan, Tajikistan will never accept Taliban in power.'

There has been no encouragement at any level from Washington on a regional conference. Taking that route entails the risk of losing control, what with Iran being an unavoidable part of such a regional enterprise. A UNSC resolution directing a process in Afghanistan may well be the United States' preferred route.

Any step that focuses largely on the Taliban (Pashtun) will immediately invite North and West Afghanistan – the Tajiks, Hazaras, Uzbeks, Turkmans, who constitute 60 percent of the population – to join hands. Yes, Pashtuns are 40 percent, but they become a minority if all the others gang up. And this divide is along the largely Pashtun–non-Pashtun areas.

Should the North and the West be pushed to thwart Taliban domination, outside powers such as Iran, Uzbekistan and Russia would get directly involved in what will then be the recipe for the mother of all civil wars. Official estimates in Kabul are that in the North, on the Afghan side of Amu Darya, which divides the country from Uzbekistan, the gas deposits are in excess of 130 trillion cubic feet. This is just one of the hidden wealths of the country, which is already stoking major differences within ISAF – between, say, the Germans and the US.

A theory gaining some credence in Kabul and Mazar-e-Sharif is that major interests in Iran and Afghanistan would not like the Americans to depart. As a potential target for military action because of its alleged nuclear ambitions, Teheran retains the capacity for massive retaliation so long as Americans remain in Afghanistan, Balochistan and Iraq – just on the other side of the border.

In Afghanistan, American presence means the circulation of unbelievably large sums of money among NGOs and freelance intelligence agents. Any foreign-funded project requires security and intelligence. The result is a crisscross of countless intelligence agencies without any master-hand holding the threads. Every NGO is making money hand over fist.

Senior Americans in Kabul are not terribly hospitable to non-US or non-British journalists or writers. The level that is accessible is easily provoked into such outbursts as: 'The people who attacked the US, who are a cesspool of extremists with nuclear weapons – do you expect us to leave them to their devices?' Ironically, these negatives work out as a kind of positive marketing for Pakistan: The implication here is that the US must keep a close watch on a nation that is 'too nuclear to be allowed to fail'.

Here lies the clue to what the Americans may have in mind for the Af-Pak region. Keep improvising the script in Afghanistan, scale down troops to a level where terrorism or civil strife is kept within manageable proportions, see that natural resources are not gobbled up by other ISAF partners, or others, after all the expenditure in blood and treasure by the Americans.

An extended stay in Afghanistan, with occasional rhetoric to the contrary – and some tactical scaling down – would enable the US to keep a steady gaze on the state next door, which has sold itself as a red-hot danger. A state 'too nuclear to be allowed to fail'! Pakistan, not Afghanistan, is the big story. Of course, staying on in the Afghan bases would have the additional advantage of surveillance of Central Asia, resurgent Russia, and risen China as well.

In a lecture to the cadets of the US Marine Corps War College, Stephen Cohen of Brookings Institution said a year ago that there are now two wars being fought in South Asia: 'The first war is being fought by the United States and the International Security Assistance Force against the Taliban in Afghanistan. This is an important war, but primarily because of its impact on the second war, that is being fought by the Pakistan Army against the Pakistan Taliban and, potentially, against Taliban-like movements in Punjab and elsewhere in the state.'

This is the grim reality and the US is confronted with difficult choices. One can only hope for developments, that may force changes and bring some clarity in Washington's objectives. For the present, leading American think tanks seem to be discussing options pointing to a partition of Afghanistan – an idea forcefully projected by Ambassador Robert Blackwill. In this, he is not alone. Steve Coll, head of the New America Foundation, a think tank, also argues that Washington should be aiming at establishing alliances with regional strongmen in the North and West of the country against the Taliban in the South and East. He considers the Taliban unreliable partners.

Richard Haass, a well-known expert in foreign policy and security-related issues, rejects a 'Pashtunistan' solution as unrealistic. Attempts to strengthen Kabul and its armed forces and police, according to him, are a waste. Washington should give more support to the regional forces that oppose the al-Qaeda, keeping open room for negotiations with the Taliban who would accept this approach. He does not state where this will lead to – possibly to the multiple fracturing of Afghanistan.

Francis Fukiyama, who wrote *The End of History and the last Man* somewhat prematurely, may be on target this time. If and when the US departs (a big IF), what Afghanistan will need is a decentralized not a unitary constitution it has at present, so that the Taliban can control areas of their influence.

In all this welter, India's policy seems to carry the weight of an unspoken clarity of purpose and action. It commends itself to the people of Afghanistan including the Pashtuns – India's traditional friends – because it serves them with the objective of strengthening the country internally without 'creating trouble' as some others do. Who knows, India's 'Diplomacy by Default' may have trumped other schools of diplomacy in Afghanistan.

The United States and the Arab World

Uma Purushothaman

Introduction

The Arab world is a widespread area stretching from Morocco to Yemen, comprising Arab-speaking people in West Asia and North Africa. The US has always had a complicated and complex relationship with the Arab world and has vital interests there. The area is a source of many problems for the US and the world because of unresolved conflicts, great power politics, dictatorships, violence, radical ideologies and the presence of Weapons of Mass Destruction (WMD). The drivers of US policy in the Arab world can be divided into nine main categories and the United States' relations with each of the countries in the region are derivatives of one or the other of these drivers or a combination of these drivers.

Energy Resources

The Arab world rose in importance after the discovery and development of oil in the region in the period after the Second World War. Today countries in the region hold almost 60% of the proved oil reserves and almost 45% of proved natural gas reserves in the world.[1] It is estimated that in the coming years, these countries will supply one-third of global oil supplies and 35% of global gas needs.[2] These statistics clearly point toward the importance of the Arab countries for a world which is highly dependent on fuels derived from these sources of energy and the dominance of the region in the global energy market. This dependence is set to increase in the coming years in the absence of any new source of energy or some miracle technology. Thus, oil from the region is vital to the global economy. This is particularly true of the US, the world's largest consumer and importer of oil. The Persian Gulf states alone supplied nearly 15 percent of American petroleum imports in 2010.[3]

Another oil-related strategic interest of America, namely the capability to deny, in a situation of crisis or conflict, control or access to these vast resources of oil to an enemy is safeguarded by the USA's unchallenged supremacy in the region. The price of oil is an important domestic issue in the US. Therefore, American politicians have a vested interest in ensuring that the price of oil remains reasonable. Arising out of all this is the US interest in peace and stability in the region, because disturbances and instability in the region could lead to a hike in global oil prices, as seen during the oil crisis of 1973. The importance of the region's oil for America can be seen from estimates which say that the US spends, on average, $304.9 billion annually in 'hidden' costs due to imported oil, which include military expenditures specifically tied to defending oil in the region, the cost of lost employment and investment resulting from the diversion of financial resources, and the cost of periodic 'oil shocks'[4].

An important strategic goal of the United States in the region is to make sure that oil from the region flows freely to its allies in Europe and Asia and to the US itself. Under the existing US-led global economic and political system, the US (with help from allies and others) maintains the safety and unhindered flow of world trade. Due to the American umbrella, countries like Germany, Japan, China, Korea and India do not need to maintain the military strength to project forces into the Middle East to ensure their access to energy and provide safety for their supertankers carrying fuel.[5] For this system to work, the US has to prevent any power from dominating the region while preserving the ability to defend the safe passage of ships through the straits of Hormuz and other shipping lanes in the region.[6] Therefore, guaranteeing the safety of oil reserves and supply routes and maintaining its naval supremacy in the region will remain a critical goal of US foreign and security policies for the foreseeable future.

Oil moguls from the Arab countries have significant business interests in the US. US companies have substantial economic stakes in the region. US oil companies are involved in exploration, production, refining and transportation of oil and gas products from the region. They also have public-private oil ventures with national oil companies.[7] Petrodollars have been recycled for years into the American economy, making Arabs from the region stakeholders in many American conglomerates and companies. Oil from the region is also traded worldwide in dollars, which reinforces the US currency's credibility and stability. These interests also necessitate continuing American political and economic engagement in the region, buttressed by substantial military presence for an indefinite period.

Israel's Security and Egypt

Israel and the US are the closest of allies, cooperating on a wide range of issues. Since Israel's creation in 1948, the United States has emphasised its historic and moral commitment to ensure the continued existence of the Jewish homeland in the region by helping Israel to maintain "its margin of security"[8] as it coped with antagonistic Arab neighbours. Israel is the only functioning democracy in the region and is pro-US in its foreign policy orientation. Moreover, Israel is an important domestic issue in the US because of the influence of the Jewish lobby. The US commitment to Israel's security and survival is possibly the one consistent theme in US foreign policy towards the region through every administration, Republican or Democrat. As President Carter once said, 'It is absolutely crucial that no one in our country or around the world ever doubt that our number one priority in the Middle East is to protect the right of Israel to exist, to exist permanently.'[9] The US has disbursed more economic and military assistance to Israel than to any other country. While during the Cold War, Israel was a key ally in countering the spread of Soviet influence in the region, today it is a key ally in the fight against terrorism and in counter-proliferation. It is also an important counterpoint to Iran's influence in the region. Therefore, the security of Israel is one of the most important strategic interests and reasons for continuing US engagement in the region.

One of the strategies that the US adopted to ensure Israel's security was to align with Egypt. Egypt has strategic importance, of its own due to its control over the Suez Canal, its leadership role in the Arab world and because of its importance in promoting peaceful ties between Israel and the Arab countries. Israel is an integral part not only of the US-Egypt relationship, but also of Washington's relations with other Arab capitals. During much of the Cold War, Washington's relations with Egypt were less than cordial as the latter was more pro-Soviet than pro-West. This changed in 1979 when Anwar Sadat signed a peace treaty with Israel at Camp David, brokered by President Carter. After that, Egypt became one of the largest recipients of US aid. Military cooperation with the US helped Egypt modernise its armed forces. The Egyptian-Israeli peace treaty strengthened America's dominant position in the region, ensured that Egypt became a regional stabiliser, facilitated Egypt becoming a market economy and ended Israel's isolation in the region.[10]

US military and economic assistance to Egypt guaranteed continued Egyptian adherence to the 1979 Egypt-Israel peace treaty (thereby helping to secure Israel), sustaining America's influence in Egypt as well as among Egypt's moderate Arab and African friends (thus contributing to regional stability) and also serves as a means of continued access to the region's oil reserves, trade opportunities and military bases.[11] Egypt also took part in Operation Desert Storm against Iraq and after 9/11, it became a close ally in the war against terrorism.

Egypt's strategic location at the crossroads of the Arab world, Africa and the Mediterranean region and its large military are vital elements within the Pentagon's planning for the whole of the 'CENTCOM' area, which includes the battlefield of Afghanistan, the Persian Gulf, Iraq and Iran.[12] However, since the fall of the Mubarak regime during the first phase of the Arab Spring, relations between the two countries have entered an era marked by a degree of uncertainty. The Egyptian government, led by its military, has blamed the West for the continuing unrest in the country. Also, Islamists belonging to the Muslim Brotherhood (MB), generally regarded as anti-West, won in the parliamentary elections held after Hosni Mubarak's overthrow. Egypt has moved ahead with the trial of 19 Americans, one of them the US Transportation Secretary's son, on charges of illegal funding of Egyptian non-profit organisations. Though the US had generally supported the revolution and Mubarak's ouster, Washington responded to these recent occurrences with threats of stopping all aid, including military aid to Egypt. The election of an MB member to the presidency may yet cause more ripples in the relationship. However, both Cairo and Washington are conscious of the mutuality of their interests and interdependence.

American Military Bases

The existence of US military bases in the region is a reality for the long term. Though originally built to protect American oil interests, the bases have become self-perpetuating as they also help the US to maintain its hegemony in the region, to protect its allies against attacks and to project its power. The US' defence treaties with several countries in the region are meant to ensure their stability as oil-producing countries and allow the US to have bases in the region, to hold military exercises, to sell arms, etc. [13] The US has bases in Qatar, Bahrain, Oman, Morocco and Kuwait. The two largest airbases of the United States are in Qatar and the UAE.[14] The base in Saudi Arabia was shut down in 2003, when its troops quit the country because of the growing resentment against foreign troops from the locals.

The US Navy's Fifth Fleet, based in Bahrain since 1948, plays an important part in providing security to the Gulf, in containing nearby Iran and keeping an eye on piracy. The base in Manama allows the US military to protect Saudi oil installations and the Gulf waterways used to protect oil transport, without any sensitive presence of American troops on Saudi soil.[15] Bahrain also provides basing and over-flight clearances for US aircraft engaged in Afghanistan and helps cut off financing for terrorists.[16] Similarly, the UAE regularly hosts port calls and shore visits for American naval vessels and permits the US military to use Al Dhafra air base for supporting many missions in the CENTCOM's area of operations.[17] All this constitutes a significant US military presence in the region, which should be expected to continue indefinitely as the smaller Arab states of the Gulf region view it as necessary to counter Iran's influence.

Containing Iran and Preventing the Spread of WMDs

The US has said that its policy towards the states of the Arabian peninsula focusses on 'working with the Gulf nations to increase cooperation to address security issues of mutual concern.'[18] One of the main security interests of the US in the region is countering the influence of Iran and stopping its nuclear weapons programme. Iran has an ambitious missile programme, which complements its nuclear programme and has built what is reportedly the biggest ballistic missile inventory in the region. So, the US today sees Iran as the primary source of instability and insecurity in the region.

The US and Iran have had no direct trade ties since 1995, when the US banned all commercial and financial transactions between American companies and Iranian public and private entities because of its attempts to develop WMDs. Iran supported the United States during its war against the Taliban regime in

Afghanistan in 2001 as well as during the diplomatic efforts that followed, like the Bonn conference. Despite this, President George W. Bush declared Iran to be a member of the 'axis of evil', effectively foreclosing any chance of reconciliation.

Iran's support for Hezbollah in Lebanon and Hamas in the Palestinian territories (especially Gaza) has also played a role in thwarting better US-Iran relations. Despite the war of words between Iran and the US, there are some areas where clearly there is a correspondence of interests, like in preventing the Taliban's return to power in Afghanistan. Nevertheless, the US-Iran standoff continues, although the Obama administration began a process that led, in October 2009, to direct negotiations with the Iranian leadership, though nothing concrete has happened since then, and in fact, relations worsened when the US imposed further sanctions on Iran in 2012 in addition to freezing all Iranian government assets in American territory. In response, Iran threatened to block the Strait of Hormuz through which a substantial amount of the world's oil passes, though it has not yet carried out this threat.

The US sees the Arab states, particularly the Persian Gulf states, as allies to balance against Iran. Iran has frequently criticised the Gulf Cooperation Council (GCC) countries for their regimes' pro-American leanings, has territorial disputes with the UAE over three islands in the Persian Gulf, and has even laid claim over Bahrain saying that it was part of the Persian Empire. The loss of Iraq as their bulwark against Iran after the US toppled Saddam Hussein's regime has further accentuated uneasiness about Iran's growing influence in the GCC countries. There is thus a convergence of interests between the US and the GCC countries as the ruling regimes in the region – which are all Sunni – see Shia Iran, and its influence among the region's Shia minorities as threat to their stability and survival.

The GCC countries fear that Iran's goal is to become the regional hegemon. In addition to a direct attack from Iran, they are also worried about Iran's 'power projection, which includes the soft power of religious and political propaganda among the Shias and wider Arab opinion, along with armed intervention' through proxies like Hizbollah and Hamas in Lebanon and Gaza.[19] The George W. Bush administration gave great importance to forming a coalition against Iran by augmenting the Gulf States' defence structures.[20] The Obama administration is building on President Bush's commitments to deploy anti-missile defence systems and accelerate hardware sales to the GCC countries to build an alliance against Iran. It has stepped up arms sales to the Persian Gulf states and improved defences for their oil installations.[21] Arms sales have been justified as 'deterrence against Iranian expansionism and Iranian aggression in the future'.[22] Similarly, though Israel and the countries of the Persian Gulf have fought wars with each other, today they share with the US the same strategic interest of fighting radical extremism and dealing with Iran.

WMDs in the region are a real threat to US allies as well as its forces positioned in various bases around the region. This explains Washington's uncompromising stance against WMDs in the region. Iran has biological weapons and is moving towards acquiring nuclear weapons. Iran's historic animosity towards Israel means that it could use such weapons against Israel. The Middle East did actually witness the use of chemical weapons in the Iran-Iraq War. Moreover, Syria allegedly has vast stocks of chemical weapons. The US further suspects Syria of working with Iran to develop WMDs. In 2003, the US began the process of normalising relations with Libya only after Libya renounced terrorism and cooperated with the US and the International Atomic Energy Agency (IAEA) in getting rid of its WMDs. The US terminated the applicability of the Iran-Libya Sanctions Act to Libya on 23 April 2004, ended economic sanctions against the country and removed it from the list of state sponsors of terrorism.

Economic Relations

The US has FTAs with several countries such as Morocco, Israel, Jordan, Bahrain and Oman. The countries of the Persian Gulf also have large stakes in the American economy because of their investments in dollar-denominated assets.[23] In 2008, the Middle East and North African (MENA) countries together constituted the fourth largest export market for the US and total bilateral trade was worth US$215 billion.[24] Major US exports are manufactured goods, machinery and transport equipment, food and chemicals. Among the countries in the region, the UAE is the top importer of US goods and services. The US-Arab Chamber of Commerce has projected that US exports to the Arab world will reach $117 billion in 2013. However, the US share of the Middle East export market has been declining over the last few years while that of China is increasing. In 2008, MENA countries together ranked as the fifth largest supplier of imports to the US, and major items were Mineral Fuel and Oil (crude), Precious Stones and Pharmaceutical products.[25] At the same time, US FDI to the region, particularly in infrastructure, is growing. Arms sales are a substantial part of US-Arab trade relations.

Market for American Weapons

The Arab countries are major buyers of arms from the US. In recent years, Saudi Arabia and Kuwait in particular have bought significant amounts of arms from the US. In 2009, while Saudi

Arabia bought arms worth $1.7 billion, Kuwait's arms purchases amounted to $200 million; in 2009, Saudi Arabia also got deliveries of arms worth $2.7 billion while Kuwait reached an agreement to buy arms worth $1.6 billion.[26] From 2002–2009, Saudi Arabia was first among other countries in buying US arms, signing deals worth 39.9 billion dollars, followed by India (32.4 billion dollars), the UAE (17.3 billion dollars) and Egypt (13.9 billion dollars).[27] Arms purchases by these countries have strengthened their defence and strategic ties with the US and enhanced interoperability with American forces. Also, as the arms industry employs a large number of people, these deals are important for the US economy.

Great Power Rivalry

The entry of China in the region in recent years has led to the US strengthening its own presence there. China's involvement in the region started primarily because of its increased consumption of oil to sustain its economic growth. It has floated several oil and gas companies such as China Petroleum & Chemicals Corporation (SINOPEC), China National Petroleum Corporation (CNPC), and China National Offshore Oil Company (CNOOC) for acquiring hydrocarbon assets and for facilitating oil and gas contracts in the future. China also engages at several levels with Iran, Syria and Turkey, all of which have had less than cordial relations with the US in recent times. It has invested heavily in oil and gas fields in Iran as well as Iraq, and is strengthening its military ties with the region in order to protect its oil interests and gain influence. China's growing economic foothold has translated into a military foothold as well, due to the large-scale participation of Chinese army personnel in energy projects and the strategic partnerships that it has with important states in the region.[28] China already has a history of supplying missile technology to Egypt, Syria and Libya and colluding in Algeria's nuclear programme.[29,30]

Even as it strengthens ties with the Arab states, China is deepening its ties with Iran; it is Iran's biggest trading partner. China has been supplying arms, including missiles and aircraft, to Iran since 1981. For China, Iran's importance arises out of it being the only energy supplier in the Gulf that it can reach through pipelines as well as sea routes, thus ensuring a diversification of supply lines in the event of a blockade or foreign interdiction campaign against China to cut off its energy supplies.[31] Also, some commentators suggest that China sees Iran as a potential ally in its strategic rivalry with the US.[32] Though China has supported the sanctions on Iran, it is unlikely to completely stop all dealings with Iran. The growing Chinese footprint in the Middle East is likely to lead to the strengthening of US presence in the region.

While the US has said that its focus over the next years will be the Indo-Pacific and not the Middle East, clearly it is not going to withdraw from the region in a hurry given that its place could be taken over by China or Russia. This is clearly articulated in the Pentagon's defence Strategic Guidelines released in January 2012 which says that '...the United States will continue to place a premium on US and allied military presence in – and support of – partner nations in and around this region'.[33]

Fight Against Terrorism and Promotion of Democracy

After 9/11, the fight against terrorism became the overarching premise of deepening US security relations with the region. Most of the countries in the region became allies in the US war on terror. Saudi Arabia, for instance, acted against the al-Qaeda in the country and against financing of terrorists. Similarly, Kuwait also became an important partner in the war and provided assistance in the military, diplomatic and intelligence arenas and also helped to block financing of terrorist groups. Likewise, Israel and Egypt also allied with the US in this fight. Yemen became important because of the American need for its cooperation and support for fighting the al-Qaeda in the Arabian Peninsula (AQAP) in Yemen. The US gave military and economic aid to Yemen and launched drone attacks against the al-Qaeda targets in the country. As Wikileaks cables show, President Saleh covered up for the US saying these attacks were carried out by the Yemeni air force.

Tunisia is an important ally in the fight against terrorism and cooperates in NATO's Operation Active Endeavour, which provides counterterrorism surveillance in the Mediterranean. Algeria is an important partner in the fight against groups linked to the al-Qaeda in North Africa like the al-Qaeda in the Islamic Maghreb (AQIM). It receives security assistance from the US and there is close military-to-military cooperation between the two countries. Morocco is a major non-NATO ally and an important partner of the US in the war against terror.

The US, under President George W. Bush, saw democracy as the best way to counter the influence of radical Islam in the region. However, President Obama has made it clear that democracy cannot be imposed from above and should come from the grassroots. He has emphasised on Internet freedom and access to technology, governance as opposed to democracy programming and downplayed US leadership in democracy promotion. Aid for civil society and for promoting better governance has continued under President Obama. During the recent upheavals in the region, the US indicated support for the democratic protests. In a speech in May 2011[34] President Obama said that the US not only supports, but will use all the diplomatic, economic and strategic tools at its disposal to promote political and economic reforms in the region. He promised support to countries during their transitions to democracy and has promised to engage with the people rather than the elites. His speech is recognition of the fact that Washington's support to dictators had contributed to anti-Americanism in the region and damaged America's credibility among the people. He has reached out to the new political forces that have emerged in the countries ruled by dictators. Monarchies in the region continue to be US allies and the Kings, Sheikhs and Amirs seem to have better support from the people for reasons of traditional loyalties and tribal bonds.

Protection of Strategic Routes

Transit between Asia and Europe requires the use of the air space and sea space of several Arab countries. The United States' status as a great power is dependent, to a large extent, on its ability to ensure a secure environment for its armed forces to travel and to project power not only in the region, but also in other places. Therefore, it has to have close cooperation with the countries in the region to guarantee access to their sea and air space. So the US has had a strong naval presence in the region since 1971.

Conclusion: A Region in Transformation

The Arab world is today in the throes of a major transformation and the Arab Spring will probably bring in more transparency, more frequent elections and more accountability to the people even in countries where regimes have not fallen. In Egypt and Libya, much uncertainty still prevails and there is continuing violence and turmoil in Syria. US efforts, directed through the

UN, to resolve the crisis have been thwarted by Chinese and Russian vetoes and non-cooperation. It is going to take some time to establish institutions of democracy. A period of political instability is unavoidable, for the region is in a state of unparalleled transformation today, creating a new strategic space and a new Arab order.

The US has suffered some setbacks in the region, and while the new regimes, where dictators have fallen, might not coordinate polices as closely with the US as in the past, surviving monarchical regimes would certainly have taken note of the United States' abandonment of allies like Mubarak. But while the US has now made it clear that it does not want to be seen as supporting despots against the people's movements, it is in a much better position than any other country to goad and help the monarchies, with their hallowed traditions and tribal linkages, to reform themselves.

The main points of America's engagement in the region in the future will probably be based on support for democratic transitions and economic development, safeguarding Israel's security, non-proliferation of WMDs, peace and stability in the region, maintaining its preponderance in the region and supporting regional security. The nature of these interests is so enduring that the US has no option but to remain engaged and maintain a significant military presence in the region for a long time to come.

The United States in Central Asia

Angira Sen Sarma

The independence of the five Central Asian Republics (CARs) in 1991 gave the United States the opportunity to engage directly with them. Both strategic and economic interests have been instrumental in guiding US policy towards this region – endowed with rich natural resources, especially hydrocarbons. Access to energy resources is one of the prime US interests in the region. Also, with Russia, China, Iran and Afghanistan as neighbours, the region is strategically significant for the US. Even after US troops move out of Afghanistan, the US will continue to engage with the CARs, for energy needs as also for strategic and economic reasons.

Various issues have from time to time influenced US policy towards the region. Immediately after independence of the CARs, the US interests in the region included primarily the safety of nuclear weapons and materials, non-proliferation, access to energy resources, promotion of free markets and democracy, peace and stability. Post 9/11 and with the beginning of the 'Operation Enduring Freedom' in Afghanistan, US partnership with the CARs witnessed a new beginning.

The Afghanistan Factor

Geographic proximity between Central Asia and Afghanistan made cooperation of the CARs crucial for the US war effort in Afghanistan. Three of the five CARs (Turkmenistan, Tajikistan and Uzbekistan) share borders with Afghanistan. Charles William Maynes has rightly observed:

> September 11 abruptly brought the United States and Central Asia together much more closely and permanently. One of the world's richest countries, a state so powerful that its military and economic reach seems limitless, suddenly began to voice greater concern over developments in one of the world's most remote and powerless regions. Of course, Washington's heightened interest is understandable. If Central Asian countries take the wrong path, it is feared, they may willingly or unwittingly provide sanctuary to the kinds of terrorists that struck the Pentagon and the World Trade Centre[1].

President Bush, after the September 11 attack, announced that the United States is dependent on 'critical support' of countries such as Pakistan and Uzbekistan[2] for its mission in Afghanistan. Highlighting the importance of the CARs for the US mission in Afghanistan, the former Assistant Secretary of State for European and Eurasian Affairs, Elizabeth Jones, said in 2001 that the CARs would play a 'critical role' in the campaign against terrorism[3]. After 9/11, barring Turkmenistan, the other Central Asian states came forward to assist the US in its war effort in Afghanistan. The opening of the US bases at Karshi Khanabad (K2) in Uzbekistan and at Manas in Kyrgyzstan brought the region closer to the US. The CARs also had vital stakes in maintaining peace and stability in Afghanistan, which made them cooperate with the US. In addition, the CARs received huge financial assistance from the US for their support. Martha Brill Olcott, a noted expert on Central Asia, argues that the post September 11 'security environment created an unexpected second chance for the Central Asian states'[4].

Washington's influence in the region suffered a major blow after the Andijan incident and the closure of the K2 base in 2005. The continuing crisis in Afghanistan, however, has encouraged the US to re-engage with the CARs. William J. Burns, the US Under Secretary of Political Affairs, stated in his remarks at the US Chamber of Commerce in 2009, that cooperation from the CARs is essential to tackle global challenges like drug trafficking, maintaining stability in Afghanistan, etc. The opening of the Northern Distribution Network (NDN) in 2009 as an alternative route to transport materials to the coalition forces stationed in Afghanistan emphasises the role the CARs play in stabilising Afghanistan. With the coalition's main supply lines through Pakistan under constant threat from the Taliban, an alternative supply route became essential. The new overland route is a 'commercially based logistical corridor connecting Baltic and the Black Sea ports with Afghanistan via Russia, Central Asia and Caucasus'[5]. The route is used for the transport of non-lethal goods from Latvia through Russia, Kazakhstan and Uzbekistan to northern Afghanistan. Indicating the importance of the region, the US Assistant Secretary, Bureau of South and Central Asian Affairs, Robert Blake, said in his testimony before the House Foreign Affairs Committee: 'Central Asia plays a vital role in our Afghanistan strategy. A stable future for Afghanistan depends on the continued engagement of its Central Asian neighbours – just as a stable, prosperous future for the Central Asian states is linked to bringing peace, stability and prosperity to Afghanistan'[6].

Access to Energy Resources

Endowed with rich natural resources, especially hydrocarbon reserves, the CARs have attracted worldwide attention since their independence. Access to the region's energy resources is one of the prime drivers of US policy towards the region. Three of the five CARs (Kazakhstan, Turkmenistan and Uzbekistan) are rich in hydrocarbon reserves.

The table below compares the hydrocarbon reserves of the CARs, Russia and the Middle East.

Table 1: Proven Oil and Gas Reserves

Country	Proven Oil Reserves at end of 2010 (thousand million barrels)	% Share of total world production	Proven Gas Reserves at end of 2010 (in trillion cubic metres)	% Share of total world production
Kazakhstan	39.8	2.9	1.8	1.0
Turkmenistan	0.6	Less than 0.05	8.0	4.3
Uzbekistan	0.6	Less than 0.05	1.6	0.8
Russian Federation	77.4	5.6	44.8	23.9
Middle East	752.5	54.4	75.8	40.5

Source: B.P. Statistical Review of World Energy, June 2011 [Online: Web] Accessed 31 October. 2011, URL: http://www.bp.com/assets/bp_internet/globalbp/globalbp_uk_english/reports_and_publications/statistical_energy_review_2011/STAGING/local_assets/pdf/statistical_review_of_world_energy_full_report_2011.pdf

Reserves of the CARs constitute 3 percent and 6.1 percent, respectively of the global oil and gas reserves. Kazakhstan has the largest oil reserves and Turkmenistan accounts for the largest gas reserves in the region. Oil and gas reserves of the Middle East constitute 54.4 percent and 40.5 percent, respectively of the total oil and gas reserves of the world. The Central Asian reserves are rather moderate and will not be able to replace the world's dependence on the Middle East. Nevertheless, these republics can serve, to some extent, as an alternative source of oil and gas.

Oil and gas have often been used by states as weapons in international conflicts. These are 'two major strategic resources' and their security is of prime importance[7]. The US, like other countries, has been looking for alternative sources of oil to reduce its dependence on the Middle East. The Silk Road Strategy Acts of 1999 and 2006 identified access to energy resources as one of the important US objectives in the region. The 1999 Act (Section 2) says, 'the region of the South Caucasus and Central Asia could produce oil and gas in sufficient quantities to reduce the dependence of the United States on energy from the volatile Persian Gulf region'. The 2006 Act (Section 101) says, 'It is the policy of the United States to assist the countries of Central Asia and Caucasus for energy and energy transit'. Section 201 of the 2006 Act highlighted that the 'Pressing need for diversification of energy resources makes access to Central Asia and Caspian Sea oil and gas resources a high energy security priority of the United States'. The appointment of Richard Morningstar as the Special Envoy for Energy to Central Asia in 2009 reflects the US interest in the region's energy sector.

With the region opening to the outside world in 1991, pipeline politics intensified. The US energy objectives in the region include building multiple pipeline routes bypassing Russia and China.

As part of the Soviet legacy, all pipelines linking Central Asia to international markets pass through Russia. Since the independence of these republics, other players like the US and China are actively engaged in constructing pipelines bypassing Russia. Section 202 of the 2006 Silk Road Strategy Act mentioned that the US energy interests in the region also include 'Preventing any other country from establishing a monopoly on energy resources or energy transport infrastructure in the countries of Central Asia and the South Caucasus that may restrict United States access to energy resources'. Central Asia (along with the Caucasus, the Black Sea and the Balkans) has emerged as geo-strategically significant 'either as oil and gas producing regions or as strategic transport routes'[8]. The US energy interests in the region also include controlling production and pipeline routes for safe transportation of oil and gas to western markets[9]. Some of the US-supported pipelines to reduce CARs' dependence on the Russian pipeline system are Baku-Tibilisi-Ceyhan (BTC), Nabucco and Turkmenistan-Afghanistan-Pakistan-India (TAPI). Except for the BTC, none of the pipelines have materialised so far. On the other hand, China has emerged as a powerful player in the region after the successful implementation of the two pipelines carrying Central Asian oil and gas to China.

Russia and the China Factor

Geo-political competition in Central Asia is one of the important determinants of US policy towards the region. The end of Soviet rule created a power vacuum in the region, which became the center of power politics among various players like Russia, the US, China and others. Obviously, the contiguity of Russia and China to the Central Asian states would play a significant role in shaping US policy toward the region.

Russia remains an important player in the region despite differences with the CARs and their eagerness to reduce dependence on Russia. Russia enjoys a dominant position in the region's energy sector because of the existing Soviet-era pipelines. Russia is one of the top trading partners of the CARs and a large number of labourers from CARs migrate to Russia for jobs. A sizable Russian population in these republics, prevalence of the Russian language, presence of Russian troops in the border regions and defence cooperation with Russia are other factors strengthening Russian influence in the region.

In the last few years, China has considerably strengthened its position and has emerged as an important economic player in the region. Three of the five CARs (Kazakhstan, Kyrgyzstan and Tajikistan) share borders with China. CARs and China have resolved their border disputes amicably, which were part of the Sino-Soviet border problems. The quest for energy is one of the primary interests driving China to the region. Central Asian oil and gas have already started flowing to China, which has given it a strong foothold in the region. China has also become one of the important trading partners of the CARs. In addition to access to energy resources, China is also interested in preventing the Uighur separatist movement in the Xinjiang autonomous region from gaining support of the Turkic people of Central Asia.

Russian and Chinese presence in Central Asia will impinge on the United States' long-term interest in the region, especially in the energy sector. These two big neighbours of the CARs have further strengthened their position in the region through the Shanghai Cooperation Organisation (SCO), a regional grouping consisting of Russia, China, Kazakhstan, Kyrgyzstan, Tajikistan and Uzbekistan. The group, since its inception, has denied membership to the US. Russian and Chinese efforts to use the SCO forum to weaken US influence in the region was evident at the Astana Summit of 2005, which had asked for a definite time for withdrawal of US troops from the region.

Nuclear Non-Proliferation

During the Soviet period, nuclear materials and weapons were located in the CARs, and these had remained in the republics after their independence. The presence of nuclear materials in these republics was a concern for the international community.

Uranium reserves are also abundant in the region, which was also the site for many Soviet nuclear, biological, chemical, radiological weapons and missile tests. For example, the Vozrozhdeniye Island, lying between Kazakhstan and Uzbekistan in the Aral Sea was the largest testing site for biological weapons. Proper safeguarding of the WMD materials was a mammoth task for these republics and for the international community. The danger became more challenging after 2001 with the constant threat that al-Qaeda might smuggle out these materials from the region for its nefarious purposes.[10]

Denuclearisation and non-proliferation were important US objectives in the region, especially in the years following the CARs independence. The Freedom Support Act of 1992 mentioned the need for 'nuclear safety and demilitarisation to prevent nuclear accidents and the spread of nuclear weapons'. The Act also expanded the scope of the $500 million given to the US Department of defence in 1991 'To support defence conversion, non-proliferation efforts, nuclear weapons dismantlement, addressing the 'brain drain' problem, the relocation of former Soviet military forces, and nuclear plant-safety'.

The US has been assisting the CARs through various programmes to destroy their WMD materials. The Cooperative Threat Reduction (CTR) programmes was a milestone in this effort. In 2002, the United States engaged private companies to separate low-enriched uranium from uranium concentrate at Ulba Metallurgy Plant. The US allocated $6 million to decontaminate areas ofVozrozhdeniye Island and to dismantle testing infrastructure. The US, in 2004, repatriated 11 kg of fresh HEU fuel assemblies from Tashkent to Russia.[11] The US Department of Energy (DOE) has also been assisting these countries to destroy their nuclear facilities. For example, the DOE helps Kazakhstan with long-term storage facilities. The DOE in the budget for the financial year 2008 had requested for US$31.7 million to help Kazakhstan with storage facilities[12].

The US objective to denuclearise the region has been achieved. Today, the five CARs are signatories to major international non-proliferation treaties. A significant initiative reflecting the CARs' willingness to destroy their WMD materials was the signing of the Central Asia Nuclear Weapon-Free Zone (CANWFZ) treaty on 21 March 2009.

Democratisation, Human Rights and Islamic Extremism

The principal guiding documents of US policy towards Central Asia – the Freedom Support Act 1992 and the Silk Road Strategy Acts of 1999 and 2006 – have identified promotion of democracy as the main official US policy objective towards the region. The former Deputy Secretary of State, Strobe Talbott, in his famous speech – 'A Farewell to Flashman: American Policy in the Caucasus and Central Asia' – in 1997 said that the US has a 'stake' in the success of political and economic reforms in Caucasus and Central Asia. According to Talbott, 'If economic and political reform does not succeed, if internal and cross border conflicts simmer and flare, the region could become a breeding ground of terrorism, a hot-bed of religious and political extremism, and a battleground for outright war. It would matter profoundly to the United States if that were to happen in an area that sits on as much as 200 billion barrels of oil.' The Silk Road Strategy Act of 1999 had also stated that the US policy towards the region is 'to promote and strengthen independence, sovereignty, democratic government, and respect for human rights'. Progress in democratic reforms and human rights situation were officially stated as the criteria for US assistance to these republics.

The debate between democracy versus security has featured frequently in the US policy towards the region. Post 9/11, the US has often compromised democracy over security in Central Asia, raising doubts about the sincerity of its commitment to those principles. For example, after Uzbekistan became a key partner of the US in its war effort in Afghanistan, it received the highest amount of US assistance, despite reports of violations of human rights and lack of progress in political and economic reforms. Under the Foreign Military Financing (FMF) assistance, Uzbekistan's share increased from US$ 2.45 million in 2001 to US$ 36 million in 2002[13]. As reflected in the last twenty years, democracy and human rights principles will remain secondary in Washington's relations with the CARs.

The rise of Islamic extremism is another issue drawing US attention to the region. The growth of radical groups like the Islamic Movement of Uzbekistan (IMU), Hizb ut-Tahrir (HUT) and similar other groups have been threatening the stability of the region. After IMU attacks on Uzbekistan in 1999, the US blacklisted IMU as a terrorist outfit in 2000. The radical elements in Central Asia might find sympathisers from the Taliban forces in Afghanistan, similar to the support they had received from the Taliban-ruled Afghanistan. Today, resurgence of the Taliban, continuing instability and drug trafficking in Afghanistan add to the threats posed by the extremists groups in Central Asia, which have raised deep concerns in the international community.

Bilateral Relations

Kazakhstan

Kazakhstan has emerged as a significant partner of the US in the region. President Nazarbayev in his 2006 address to the nation highlighted the nature of Kazakhstan-US bilateral relations in the following words:

> Kazakhstan and the USA have built relations of a long term and stable partnership which are characterised by a broad range of cooperation on issues of international energy stability and security, the fight against terrorism and religious extremism, and further democratic transformations. The agenda for our relationship includes further development of economic cooperation, creating favourable conditions for attracting American investments and introducing advanced technologies to Kazakhstan.[14]

Given the rich hydrocarbon reserves of the Republic, the focus of the bilateral partnership is energy. The country has the potential to 'emerge as one of the three largest contributors to non-OPEC oil supply'.[15] With the region's largest oil reserves and second-largest gas reserves, Kazakhstan's cooperation is vital for the success of the US-supported pipelines in the region bypassing Russia and China. To strengthen cooperation in the energy sector, both countries established the US-Kazakhstan Energy Partnership in 2001. Various US companies are engaged in the Kazakh energy sector since the end of Soviet rule. American companies, Chevron and ExxonMobil, operate the two largest projects in the oil and gas sector – Tengiz and the North-Caspian project (Kashagan).

In the first half of 2007, US FDI was 24.6% of the total FDI in Kazakhstan.[16] About 11 percent of the total FDI in Kazakhstan in 2008 came from US companies.[17] US companies have invested about $14.3 billion in Kazakhstan since 1993, mainly in the oil and gas sector, business services, telecommunications, and electrical energy.[18] Kazakhstan is the United States' largest trade partner in the region. From US$ 35.5 million in 1992, bilateral trade increased to US$ 2602.7 million in 2010.[19]

Safety of the WMD materials in the region was one of the main US concerns in the region. Among the five CARs, Kazakhstan drew the maximum US attention because of its huge nuclear stockpiles. Kazakhstan possessed 1410 Soviet strategic missiles armed with nuclear warheads.[20] Semipalatinsk in Kazakhstan during the Soviet days tested 456 nuclear devices and radiological weapons.[21] The US, through various programmes, has assisted Kazakhstan to destroy its nuclear facilities.

The US-Kazakhstan cooperation in security and non-proliferation is one of the important factors in expanding relations between the two countries. NATO's Partnership for Peace (PfP) programmes in the region was an initiative to strengthen US geo-political influence in the region. Kazakhstan has actively participated in the NATO PfP program, which it joined in 1994. Kazakhstan started participating in the PfP Planning and Review Process (PARP) in 2002. In 2004, Kazakhstan developed its first Individual Partnership Action Plan (IPAP) under NATO-Kazakhstan cooperation.

Kazakhstan and the United States share similar views on many security-related issues. Kazakhstan has supported the US-led 'Operation Enduring Freedom' in Afghanistan. Both are worried about the growth of extremist groups in the region and are willing to cooperate on counterterrorism measures. The Republic had supported the Operation Iraqi Freedom and sent troops to Iraq. In 2005, the US Central Command conducted around 45 bilateral military cooperation events with the Ministry of Defence of Kazakhstan and other agencies, an increase of more than 100% since 2002[22]. These events included both information exchanges and military exercises.

Kazakhstan has emerged as a key player in the region and cooperation with Kazakhstan will play an important role in shaping US policy towards Central Asia. Its political stability and investment-friendly climate has been instrumental in attracting substantial foreign investments. Kazakhstan is emerging as a Eurasian power center: in 2010, it was the Chair of the Organisation for Security and Co-operation in Europe (OSCE). It is the first country from the region to assume this post, and this has boosted both its regional and international stature. In 2011 the Republic assumed the chair of the Organisation of the Islamic Conference (OIC).

Uzbekistan

US-Uzbekistan bilateral ties have gone through several changes since independence. Immediately after independence, Uzbekistan did not figure as an important country in the realm of US foreign policy making. Post 9/11, with Uzbekistan becoming a key partner in the US war efforts in Afghanistan, bilateral relations witnessed a new beginning. However, the Andijan incident and the closure of the K2 base soured relations between the two partners. Again, since 2008, mutual interests have encouraged both sides to rebuild their ties.

The security cooperation that developed after 9/11 had its genesis in the bilateral military and political cooperation of the 1990s. This has been the hallmark of the bilateral relationship. The former US Assistant Secretary of Defense, J.D. Crouch II, in his 2002 remarks to the US Senate Committee on Foreign Relations had pointed out that the US bilateral engagement with the CARs prior to September 11 had 'laid the groundwork both politically and militarily for coalition operations in Central Asia in support of the Global War on Terrorism'.[23] In February 1998, the US-Uzbekistan Joint Commission was established to facilitate regular high-level contacts and institutionalise the bilateral relations.

Prior to 9/11, security engagement with Uzbekistan mainly focused on eliminating WMD materials from the Soviet times, training of Uzbek defence personnel and military engagement within the scope of NATO PfP. Uzbekistan, while nationalising and reorganising its defence force after independence, had requested the US to train Uzbek military personnel. Uzbek defence personnel have attended several training courses, seminars and exercises supported by the US, which has been helping the Republic to eliminate its Soviet-era WMD materials. For example, Uzbekistan with US assistance decontaminated the Vorozhdeniye Island and destroyed the testing facility of chemical weapons at Nukus.

Until 2005, Uzbekistan actively participated in the NATO PfP program. In 1992, Uzbekistan joined the North Atlantic Cooperation Council (NACC) and in 1997 joined the Euro-Atlantic Partnership Council (EAPC). In 1994, Uzbekistan signed the PfP Framework Document and also a security agreement with

NATO in August 1995. Since 1996, it has been participating in various joint exercises under the 'Spirit of PfP Programme'. In June 1996, it agreed on Individual Partnership Programme (IPP) and in July 1996, it signed the PfP Status of Forces Agreement (SOFA) and its additional protocol and joined Planning and PARP in 2002. Uzbekistan remained in PARP until 2005.

The Uzbekistan-US partnership entered a new phase after 9/11, as it was the first country in the region to 'reply to Washington's call for assistance'[24] after the attack. The K2 base became a symbol of Uzbekistan-US partnership. The bilateral ties received further impetus with the signing of the Declaration on the Strategic Partnership and Cooperation Framework in March 2002. The Joint Security Cooperation Consultations signed in April 2003 was yet another effort to bring the two countries closer. The closeness between the two was evident from the huge assistance that Uzbekistan received from the US, which jumped from a mere US$14 million in 1995 to US$84.66 million in 2001 and US$297.84 million in 2002.[25]

The US presence in Uzbekistan's energy sector is negligible. The hydrocarbon reserves of Uzbekistan are moderate compared to Kazakhstan and Turkmenistan. However, Uzbekistan has the third largest gas reserves in the region, ranking 17th in the world.[26] Gazprom, the Russian gas major has the lion's share in the Republic's gas sector. Uzbekistan does not have significant oil reserves. It has only 0.6 thousand million barrels of proven oil reserves and its percentage share in the world is insignificant (See Table 1).

In 2006, the Ministry of Foreign Affairs of the Republic of Uzbekistan stated that Uzbekistan had completed 24 priority investment projects worth US$ 2383 million with investments from the US companies and assistance from financial institutions.[27] Out of this, American credits were worth US$ 1406 million,[28] while the US sources indicate the US firms have invested around US$ 500 million so far.[29] Some of the major US investors in Uzbekistan included Newmont (reprocessing gold from mining waste of the Muruntau gold mine); the Case Corporation (manufacturing and servicing cotton harvesters and tractors); Coca Cola (bottling plants in Tashkent, Namangan and Samarkand); Texaco (producing lubricants); and Baker Hughes (in oil and gas development).

At present, Uzbekistan-US economic cooperation is minimal. Closing of joint ventures like Zarafshan-Newmont has resulted in decline in the bilateral economic relations. The deterioration in the bilateral political relations has also put the economic relations between the two in trouble. Both sides are trying to mend fences. Uzbekistan supporting the Northern Distribution Network (NDN) route and allowing the US to use the cargo airport at Navoi to transport non-lethal materials to Afghanistan, and the December 2010 visit by Hillary Clinton are instances of both sides trying to rebuild their relationship.

Kyrgyzstan

The US has been assisting Kyrgyzstan to implement reforms in sectors like economy, health and education and has been supporting economic development and conflict resolution in the Ferghana Valley.[30] Kyrgyzstan became a member of the WTO in December 1998, which was supported by the US. Kyrgyzstan joined NATO's PfP programme in 1994 and in 2007 it joined the PfP PARP. The main areas of cooperation with NATO are security and peacekeeping, especially counter-terrorism cooperation and border security, crisis management and civil emergency planning[31].

US-Kyrgyzstan relations strengthened after Kyrgyzstan agreed to lease the base at Manas in 2001. The base, 30 kilometres from

Bishkek was set up in December 2001 and since then it has been one of the determining factors in the bilateral relations. The Manas airbase or the Transit Center at Manas (as it is known now) is a crucial logistical hub for the US coalition forces stationed in Afghanistan, especially after the K2 base was closed. From US$ 50 million in 1995, the total US assistance to Kyrgyzstan in 2002 increased to US$114.98 million.[32]

However, in the past years, a few incidents reflect the delicate nature of the relationship. The Manas base, which brought Kyrgyzstan closer to the US, has also been the cause of conflict between the two. In December 2006, the shooting of a Kyrgyz national by a US soldier at the base had put the relationship in trouble. The United States' reluctance to take action against the US soldier and his eventual removal from Kyrgyzstan created a rift between the two governments. The incident also dampened US popularity among the local population.

Again, in 2009, the base became an issue between the two countries. In February 2009, the former Kyrgyz President Kurmanbek Bakiyev announced that Kyrgyzstan would close down the US base at Manas, a decision which was eventually reversed. The whole episode highlighted the geo-political competition between Russia and the US in the region. Russia agreed to pay US$ 2 billion in aid to Kyrgyzstan, the same day President Bakiyev announced his decision to close the Manas base,[33] raising suspicion about Russia's role. The US finally retained the base after agreeing to increase the annual rent for the base and the amount of US assistance to Kyrgyzstan. Unlike the base at K2, the US has been paying rent for the use of the base at Manas. The Russian base at Kant established in 2003 is at a distance of over 20 kilometres from the American base at Bishkek. In 2009, Russia and Kyrgyzstan had signed an MoU for a second base in the latter country. Kyrgyzstan is the only country in the world to host both a Russian and a US base. The presence of the Russian base has made the Manas base strategically and geo-politically more significant for the US and its closure will be a blow to its image in the region.

After the interim government took over in Kyrgyzstan in 2010, the Manas Transit Center once again became a source of tension between the two countries. The interim government wanted the US to suspend the contract of the Mina Corporation, the company supplying jet fuels to the Manas base, following criminal investigations against the company. Mina Corporation and its affiliate, Red Star Enterprises, were given the contract to supply fuels in 2002. The Kyrgyz government alleges that the former President Bakiyev and his family members misused their position to gain undue profits from the company. Despite complaints from the Kyrgyz government, the US Defense Department gave a US$315-million contract to the company.[34] The US Congressional subcommittee cleared Bakiyev and his family of their involvement in any corrupt dealings, which has irked the Kyrgyz government.

With the signing of the US$630 million contract for fuel supply in 2011, the crisis seems to have ended for the time being.[35] According to the new deal, the Manas Refueling Complex, a recently established State Company, was permitted to supply 20 percent of the fuel, which in future could rise to 50 percent and the remaining requirements would be borne by the Mina Corporation and the Red Star Enterprises.[36] Although the crisis was managed temporarily, tensions prevail, which in future could strain bilateral relations. There is a feeling in Kyrgyzstan that the US is supporting Bakiyev and his cronies, which fuels misunderstanding between the two countries.

Recently, the base has been in the news again and this is

building tensions between the two countries. The new President Almazbek Atambayev after assuming power announced that all foreign troops will have to vacate the Manas base after 2014 and the US lease for the base will not be renewed beyond 2014. Since then there have been a series of negotiations between the two sides. Since February 2012 several high-level officials from the US have visited Kyrgyzstan. Some of the important visits from the US are – a delegation headed by Deputy Assistant Secretary of State for South and Central Asia, Susan Elliott, visited the Republic in February; Secretary of defence Leon Panetta visited in March; and Assistant Secretary of State for South and Central Asian Affairs, Robert Blake, and the Head of Central Command, General James Mattis, visited Kyrgyzstan in the first week of April.

Kyrgyzstan, however, has of late softened its stand on closing down the base. President Atambayev has now said that the base would be converted to a civilian transit facility, which is seen by many as a way of bargaining for a rent hike[37]. Moreover, Kyrgyzstan's Defence Council had told General Mattis during his recent visit that 'Kyrgyzstan is interested in ensuring security and stability in the country and is ready to participate fully in the efforts of the international community to assist Afghanistan. The Kyrgyz side expressed its readiness to assist the US government after 2014, but in the interests of the country, the views of the people and the security of Kyrgyzstan'.[38] Recent news reports suggest that Kyrgyzstan has also requested the US to donate its drones after it withdraws its troops from Afghanistan, which the US has agreed to consider.[39] Some observers also see the change in Kyrgyzstan's position to be a result of Russia's recent support to have NATO forces in Afghanistan beyond 2014.[40] Other developments in the region also raise questions about the future of the base. The Collective Security Treaty Organisation

(CSTO), a Russia-led security organisation in the region in its December 2011 summit meeting held at Moscow announced that no non-member country will be able to deploy military bases in the territory of the CSTO member countries without the official approval of all the members.[41] To what extent the CSTO announcement will have an impact on the Manas base remains ambiguous.

Stability in Kyrgyzstan is one of the prime US interests in the country. The prevailing grim political situation of Kyrgyzstan, social instability and fragile economic conditions could deteriorate further and destabilise the whole region. The year 2010 has been a rather tumultuous year for Kyrgyzstan. Violent street protests in April 2010 ousted Kurmanbek Bakiyev from power and an interim government headed by Roza Otunbayeva was established. In the months after the formation of the interim government, the country was faced with another crisis – the Kyrgyz-Uzbek ethnic clash in southern Kyrgyzstan. Although the government was able to tide over the crisis, tensions prevail between the two communities, which could lead to unrest in a wider area of the region.

A national referendum on 27 June 2010 made Kyrgyzstan the first parliamentary democracy in the region. The parliamentary election was held on 10 October 2010, in which none of the political parties acquired the required majority to form the government. After several rounds of negotiations, a coalition government, including the Social Democratic Party of Kyrgyzstan (SDPK), Respublika and Ata-Zhurt was formed in December 2010. Within a year, the coalition broke down and a new coalition consisting of SDPK, Respublika, Ata-Meken and Ar-Namys was established on 16 December 2010. Recent developments in the country, like rivalries between the coalition partners and the

April 2011 violence inside the Parliament, make the future of democracy uncertain in the country.

Tajikistan

Tajikistan's geographic location bordering Afghanistan and China and huge water resources make it a significant country in Central Asia.[42] The country shares the longest border with Afghanistan making it vulnerable to the situation in Afghanistan. Islamist extremism, terrorism and drug trafficking are the major threats faced by the Republic from Afghanistan. Because of its geographic location, Tajikistan acquires importance in the US strategy of maintaining peace and stability in the region. Explaining the importance of the Republic, the US government in its Congressional Budget Justification for Foreign Operations stated:

> Tajikistan is situated on the frontline of our ongoing military stabilization efforts in Afghanistan. Its own stability is undermined by a poorly managed border as well as food and energy shortages that will continue for the next few years. Support to strengthen border security, counter-narcotics efforts, democratic reforms, health, education, and economic growth is key to improving Tajikistan's role as a bulwark against regional threats such as terrorism and drugs.[43]

Tajikistan and the US established diplomatic relations in February 1992. Ever since, the primary US concern has been the country's stability. The US provided humanitarian aid and encouraged political reconciliations in Tajikistan to heal the wounds of a bloody civil war. Officials from the State Department participated as observers in the UN-brokered intra-Tajikistan peace talks.[44] Tajikistan also supported the US mission in Afghanistan after 9/11. It allowed the US to use Tajik airspace. The Dushanbe Airport was used for refuelling. The airbase could not be used for larger actions because of its limited capacity.[45] In 2009, Tajikistan allowed the US to use its territory for transiting goods like construction materials to the coalition forces in Afghanistan.[46] During the March 2012 visit to Tajikistan by General Mattis, both sides reiterated their commitments to strengthen bilateral cooperation. President Rahmon said, 'Tajikistan would like to see further strengthening of the development of ties with the United States in the sphere of security and the establishment of peace and stability in the region'.[47] The US has also agreed to continue giving assistance to the security forces of Tajikistan.[48]

Today, the bilateral cooperation includes a wide range of issues like counter-narcotics, counterterrorism, non-proliferation, regional growth and stability.[49] The US assistance to Tajikistan during the period 1992–2008 was US$778.6 million; intended mainly for humanitarian purposes.[50] It also included funds for building social, economic and political infrastructure in the Republic. Both sides signed an MoU for technical assistance to prepare legislation on micro financing. The US gave US$36 million to build a bridge on the Pyanzh River connecting Sher Khan in Afghanistan to Nizhniy Pyanzh in Tajikistan.[51] The commercial traffic started since October 2007 and about 200 trucks cross the bridge daily.[52]

Turkmenistan

Turkmenistan, until the death of President Saparmurat Niyazov, had followed a policy of positive neutrality. With Gurbanguly Berdimuhamedov assuming power in 2007, the country gradually started moving away from the policy of neutrality, which gave the US the opportunity to engage with the Republic. Turkmenistan and the US today are cooperating in many areas like border and regional security programmes, educational exchanges and English language training.[53]

The country's energy resources and its proximity to Afghanistan and Iran are the main drivers influencing US interests in Turkmenistan. According to Prof. Stephen Blank, 'Central Asia and Turkmenistan are important because of their geographical location and major energy holdings'.[54] Turkmenistan's 8 trillion cubic meters of proven gas reserves are the largest in the region (See Table 1). It accounts for 4.3 percent of the world's total gas reserves (See Table 1). Also, the US needs cooperation from Turkmenistan for the success of pipelines like Nabucco and TAPI. The country's proximity to Afghanistan makes it an important stakeholder in the Afghan peace and stability. Highlighting the importance of Turkmenistan, Richard Boucher, Assistant Secretary in the Bureau of South and Central Asian Affairs, in the State Department during his visit to Ashgabat in April 2009, stated that Turkmenistan as Afghanistan's neighbour has genuine concern about the situation in Afghanistan and a role in its stabilisation.[55] Turkmenistan's stability is also of interest to the US as unrest in this strategically located country could spill over to other Republics, which will be inimical to US interests in the region.

US-Central Asia Ties Go Beyond Afghanistan

The Afghanistan crisis, energy and geo-politics will continue to guide US engagement with the CARs. At this point, the ongoing crisis in Afghanistan will be the principal factor influencing US relations with Central Asia. Peace and stability in the region is vital for the US strategy in Afghanistan. The need for an alternate supply route to reduce dependence on Pakistan has encouraged the US to re-engage with the CARs. The new NDN route and Uzbekistan-US rapprochement reflect the importance the CARs hold for the US mission in Afghanistan. In 2009, the US started the Annual Bilateral Consultations, indicating its desire to improve and strengthen its bilateral relations with the five Republics. Dr. Murat Laumulin, a scholar from Kazakhstan has noted: 'It is in the interest of the United States to forge special relationships with Central Asian countries in order to contribute to the stability of the region'.[56]

The US objectives in the region have remained unchanged ever since the region's independence – to 'prevent the emergence of a hegemonic power in the region, promote energy and strategic partnerships that turn the region toward the West, and contribute to political and economic reforms'.[57] Even after the US pulls out its troops from Afghanistan, Central Asia will continue to attract American attention for its energy resources and Washington's larger strategic interests. Russia's old links and China's increasing influence are important considerations influencing US policy towards the region.

The CARs too have their own interests in developing close cooperation with the US. In addition to economic benefits and investments, the US presence helps these republics to balance the influence of Russia and China and prevents any one power from establishing a monopoly of presence and influence in the region. The US-CARs engagement is in mutual interest and is likely to be a long-term affair.

US Engagement with Russia

Ajish P. Joy

Once a national obsession, adversary number one and foremost foreign policy narrative, Russia has gone down several notches in the pecking order for the United States, after the collapse of the Soviet Union. The US-Russia relationship has not been smooth and the legacy of the Cold War has hampered the development of normal friendly ties between the two countries. Russia expected the West to accept it as an equal power into the western fold. However, such hopes were belied by successive US administrations as they refused to forge an alliance or partnership with Russia and treat it like a fellow great power. 'Instead, Russia has been treated as a limbless trunk of the defeated Soviet empire; a weakling and an international beggar; a petro-state not deserving its windfall profits; and a regional bully, first on probation, and then at large'.[1]

Successive US administrations have grappled with the challenge of formulating a coherent Russia policy. Bill Clinton is criticised for adopting a 'triumphalist, winner-take-all approach, including an intrusive crusade to dictate Russia's internal political and economic development; broken strategic promises, and double-standard policies impinging on Russia that presumed Moscow no longer had any legitimate security concerns abroad apart from those of the United States, even in its own neighbourhood'.[2] Bilateral ties suffered a severe setback due to the NATO campaign in Kosovo. George W. Bush started promisingly and his first meeting with Vladimir Putin in Ljubljana witnessed his famous remarks on 'getting a sense about Putin's soul by looking into his eyes'.[3] Russia announced unequivocal support for the United States in the wake of the terrorist attacks on 9/11. But things went downhill thereafter. Bush continued with his sweeping 'war on terror' and pursued a policy of democracy promotion across the world. Russia strongly disapproved of the Iraqi invasion in 2003 and the relationship further soured with the US support for 'colour revolutions' in the Russian neighbourhood. Toward the end of the Bush administration, the US-Russia relationship reached its nadir with the war in Georgia in 2008.

With a change of guard in both countries (President Dmitry Medvedev assumed office in August 2008, and Barack Obama became president in January 2009), both the United States and Russia got an opportunity to start afresh. Obama took up Russia as one of his foreign policy priorities and took a series of initiatives to improve ties with Moscow. The president in coordination with his Russian counterpart has set up the US-Russia Bilateral Presidential Commission. The Commission expects to identify areas of cooperation and pursue joint projects and actions that strengthen strategic stability, international security, economic well-being, and the development of ties between the Russian and American people. The coordinators of the Commission-Secretary

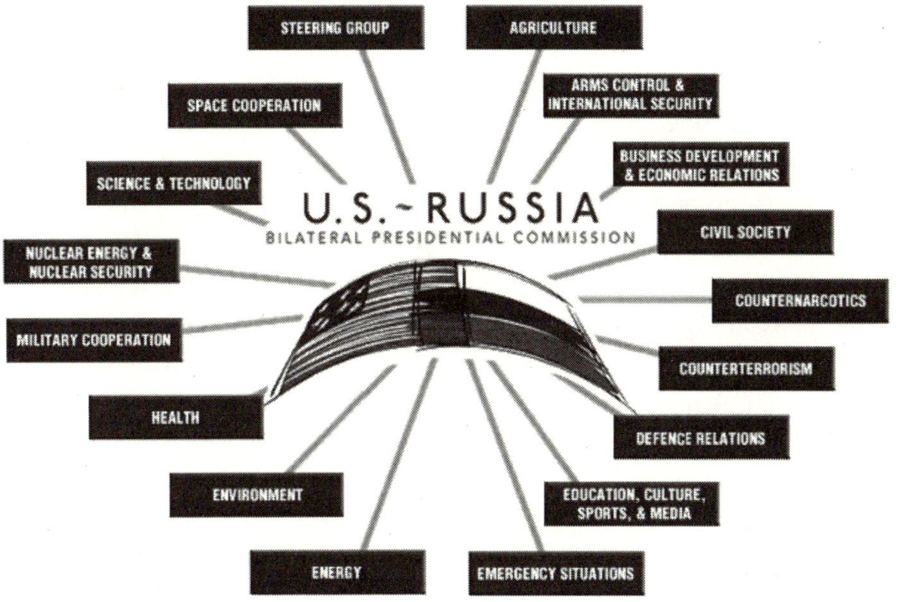

of State Hillary Clinton and Russian Foreign Minister Sergei Lavrov will meet at least once a year while the working groups and sub-committees shall meet regularly.[4]

The reset was formally announced as the new US policy by Vice President Joseph Biden during the Munich Security Conference in 2009. According to him, 'The United States and Russia can disagree and still work together where our interests coincide. And they coincide in many places.'[5]

The reset, which appeared to be working effectively for some time, faltered badly, as both countries switched on to the 'election mode'. The Russian presidential elections in March 2012 brought Putin back to the Kremlin as President; the US elections later in the year and the preceding campaign pressures, coupled with increasing divergences of opinion on a host of critical issues will not, hopefully, affect the thaw in relationship. Vladimir Putin is a proud Russian patriot and his presidency is a reality, which the US should treat with respect. The continuing unrest in the Middle East – especially in Syria – and the wave of anti-government protests, which erupted in Russia after the Duma elections in December, have all pushed the reset downhill. The new US ambassador to Russia, Michael McFaul, did not help matters when he hosted Russian Opposition figures like Just Russia Party leaders Oksana Dmitrieva and Gennady Gudkov, who were leading anti-Putin demonstrations, at the embassy in Moscow. McFaul, in fact, hosted the Opposition leaders because the visiting Undersecretary of State, Bill Burns, wanted a meeting with them. The fact that McFaul himself is a prominent pro-democracy activist, who has written a book, *Advancing Democracy Abroad: Why We Should and How We Can*, has not helped the situation. While President Medvedev sought to downplay the incident, he remarked that the ambassador should remember that he is on Russian soil and that it is important to respect Russian sensibilities. Putin and the Russian media were quick to point out that the protesters were taking orders from the US and the demonstrations were supported and orchestrated by the United States. Putin, in full election mode, launched a tirade alleging that 'Hillary Clinton has inspired the anti-government protesters; that McFaul's support for the reset is merely a fig-leaf to hide his enmity toward Moscow; and that Obama, like George Bush, deems Russia an American vassal.'[6] In the Duma, there were demands about a counterintelligence investigation into the meeting. The allegations further vitiated the atmosphere and as the election season progressed, things got worse. Notwithstanding all such negative rhetoric, it is important not to overlook the fact that over the past couple of years, the

United States and Russia have achieved some tangible progress in a few critical areas, viz. the arms control regime, management of the post Soviet space, the energy sector, and cooperation on Iran and Afghanistan.

Arms Control

US-Russia bilateral ties have been most active and visible in the field of non-proliferation and arms control. The Cold War legacy has played a role in this when the two superpowers were locked in an arms race and tried to create a system of checks and balances through a series of arms treaties. The first START aimed at reducing and limiting offensive weapons, signed by Ronald Reagan and Mikhail Gorbachev, expired in December 2009, posing a dilemma and yet presenting an opportunity to the United States and Russia in re-negotiating a more effective treaty.

After lengthy negotiations and discussions, Obama and Medvedev signed the new START in Prague in April 2010. Even after the massive reversals for the Democrats in the mid-term elections in November 2010, Obama and the Senate Majority Leader Harry Reid managed to get the treaty ratified by the US Senate on 22 December 2010 as 13 Republicans too voted with the Democrats. The Russian Parliament completed the ratification proceedings in January 2011 and the new treaty came into force on 5 February 2011.

Table 2: Comparison of the START, and the New START[7]

	START	New START
Warheads	6,000 warheads attributed to deployed ICBMs and SLBMs, and heavy bombers	1,550 deployed warheads*
Delivery Vehicles	1,600 strategic nuclear delivery vehicles (deployed ICBMs and SLBMs and their associated launchers, and heavy bombers)	700 deployed ICBMs, SLBMs, and heavy bombers equipped for nuclear armaments
		800 deployed and non-deployed ICBM and SLBM launchers and deployed and non-deployed heavy bombers equipped for nuclear armaments

*Includes warheads on deployed Intercontinental Ballistic Missiles (ICBMs) and deployed Submarine-launched Ballistic Missiles (SLBMs), and nuclear warheads counted for deployed heavy bombers.

More importantly, as Russia is trying to adapt to its relatively diminished position in the emerging global order, its nuclear arsenal is vital to Russia's national interests as it ensures Russia's strategic parity with the United States. Undoubtedly, the most notable success of the reset policy has been the conclusion of the new START treaty. This is particularly important for Russia. According to Sergei Rogov, for Russia 'the fact that the US signs such a treaty not with China or India, nor with the Europeans, reinforces the role of Russia in world affairs and confirms that Russia is still one of the leading centres of power in international arena and that its interests should be taken into consideration'.[8]

As far as the United States is concerned, having a mutually acceptable legal framework regarding the strategic nuclear weapons with Russia confers it with several advantages. It ensures 'an increased predictability in each side's nuclear activities, an increased transparency concerning each side's arsenal, an increased ability to shape future developments and an increased credibility to the US and Russian commitment under Article VI of the NPT'.[9]

The new START was not without its share of critics in the United States.The Senate Foreign Relations Committee required 21 hearings and briefings before it voted to ratify the treaty. Questions were raised about the verifiability of the new regime. Some of the critics argue that the treaty limits 'America's efforts to build missile defences, pointing to a line in the nonbinding preamble about the interrelationship between offensive and defensive strategic arms and a provision in the treaty that bans the use of missile silos or submarine launch tubes to house missile interceptors'.[10] Some of these concerns did influence the Senators, as is evident from the resolution passed by the Senate along with the ratification. The resolution mandates the administration to initiate talks with Russia on reducing its 3,800-strong tactical weapon stockpiles, landmines, artillery shells and short-range missiles, which are not covered by the new START.[11]

Further problems cannot be ruled out as the US is moving ahead with its plans to develop non-nuclear strategic options like the Conventional Prompt Global Strike (CPGS).[12] The US government has made it clear that new START does not prevent the US from deploying 'CPGS systems, and does not in any way limit or constrain research, development, testing, and evaluation of such concepts and systems'. American plans for the CPGS and the Russian response to it may perhaps shape the future of the global disarmament regime.

Another pressing concern for the US administration will be its policy concerning ballistic missile defence (BMD). While President Obama cancelled George W. Bush's missile defence plans to place interceptors in Poland and radars in the Czech Republic, he too announced his version of the missile defence regime called the European Phased Adaptive Approach,[13] a proposal accepted by NATO in its Lisbon Summit in November 2010. As part of the new plan, in May 2011 Romania agreed to host a land-based Standard Missile-3 BMD interceptor site. Soon after this announcement, the Russian Foreign Ministry issued a statement demanding legal guarantees from the United States that its missile defence shield in Romania would not target Russia's strategic nuclear forces.[14] The issue also figured prominently in the Obama-Medvedev meeting on the sidelines of the 37th G-8 Summit (26–27 May 2011) in Deauville, France. While the US clarified that the missile defence regime is to counter the Iranian threat, Moscow remains skeptical and feels that in the long term, the system could imperil Russia's arsenal and wipe-out the US-Russian power parity. According to Michael McFaul, who briefed the press about the Obama-Medvedev meeting at the G-8 Summit, Medvedev remained unconvinced about American assurances and said, 'We don't know what your technological capabilities will be in 2020'.[16] Interestingly, during NATO's Lisbon Summit, President Medvedev announced that Russia is willing to cooperate in the NATO missile defence as an 'equal partner' but chose not to explain what 'equal partnership' means. This explanation came forth in April 2011 from the Russian Deputy Prime Minister, Sergei Ivanov. According to him, under an equal partnership, the

Russians will sit along with the NATO officials 'in Brussels and agree on a red-button push to start an anti-missile, regardless of whether it starts from Poland, Russia or the UK'.[17] The top brass of the Russian military argue that in the absence of such Russian involvement in the missile defence system, Russia will be unable to launch a nuclear strike against the West after 2015, bringing to an end the Cold War balance of nuclear superpowers.[18]

Efforts at making the two parties to cooperate on the missile defence issue have been continuing. The latest such proposal mooted by the Euro-Atlantic Security Commission envisages that the three key players – the US, Russia and NATO – share data about an impending missile attack to provide 'one another with a more complete picture of any attack than countries would have on their own. But the parties would remain responsible for shooting down any missiles that threaten them. They would keep sovereign command-and-control over their own missile interceptors'.[19] The new system was developed by Henry Obering, a former chief of the US Missile defence Agency, and Viktor Esin, a former chief of staff of the Russian Strategic Rocket Forces. The new proposal was formally launched at the Munich security conference in the first week of February 2012. Putin, however, has queered the pitch by stating that the missile defence regime's sole focus is to neutralise the Russian nuclear deterrent and that Iran or North Korea do not pose a threat. The missile defence conundrum endures and it has the potential to undo all the progress made so far in the US-Russia relations.

Economic Relations

As far as economic relations are concerned, the reset has resulted in a number of American corporations like Chevron, General Electric,

Pepsi, Cisco and Alcoa investing in Russia. Aeroflot ordered Boeing 777s worth $2 billion which is expected to sustain 11,000 jobs in the United States, a major success for President Obama who all the time was bracing for a re-election battle. However, America's trade with Russia in 2010 was worth about $32 billion compared to $524 billion with Canada and $456 billion with China. Though bilateral trade between the two countries is modest, the United States can still initiate steps in ensuring Russia's integration into the global commerce, especially now that Russia has become a member of the WTO. Russia's accession to the WTO could force the US Congress to grant Russia permanent normal trade relations (PNTR) status by overturning the controversial 1974 Jackson-Vanik amendment, which has been a major irritant in the US-Russia relations.

The amendment prevents the US from giving most favoured nation status to countries that restrict emigration. A vestige of the Cold War era, it was meant to challenge the Soviet restriction on Jewish emigration. But now, with Russia joining the WTO, the US companies may be at a disadvantage as they will not be able to make full use of Russia's 'improved market access and tariff reductions, and thus be placed at a competitive disadvantage versus their European, Asian and Latin American competitors'.[20] President Obama has taken note of this issue and in his 2012 State of the Union address, he exhorted the Congress to ensure that 'no foreign company has an advantage over American manufacturing when it comes to accessing finance or new markets like Russia'.[21] However, during the presidential election campaign in 2012, the Republicans had expressed opposition to the move. The Ways and Means Committee of the Republican-controlled House has not scheduled any action yet on repealing the amendment. Meanwhile, Ros-Lehtinen, a Florida Republican who is chairman of the House Foreign Affairs Committee, has declared that he was not ready to do anything on Jackson-Vanik.[22]

On the positive side, trade negotiators from both countries managed to resolve some of the outstanding issues during the pre-WTO accession talks. The Russian side agreed to gradually put an end to the policy of giving 'trade preferences for auto parts exported to Russia's crumbling automobile industry'.[23] Russia has also agreed to tighten its intellectual property regime to boost the confidence of American IT and entertainment industries. A third agreement was regarding new standards and health protocols for the US export of poultry, pork and beef.[24] Meanwhile, with Russia's ratification of the Organization for Economic Cooperation and Development's (OECD) anti-bribery convention and its initiatives to protect anti-corruption campaigners, investors will feel more confident to do business with Russia, according to US Deputy Secretary of State William Burns.

Post Soviet Space

According to several observers, the single most important stumbling block in the healthy development of the US-Russia relations is the management of the post-Soviet space. For example, Salzman argues that 'interaction in the post-Soviet space could well be termed the Gordian knot of the US-Russian relationship'.[25] President Medvedev has explained the importance attached by Russia to the post-Soviet space. According to him, 'Russia, just like other countries in the world, has regions where it has its privileged interests. In these regions, there are countries with which Russia has friendly, cordial and historically special relations.'[26] While Medvedev refused to name these states, it was evident that he was referring to the states of the former Soviet Union (FSU).

Medvedev's statement was swiftly challenged and refuted by the US leadership including President Obama and Vice President Biden. This fundamental divergence in defining their interests in 'non zero sum game' terms in the post-Soviet space has proven to be a challenge to both Russia and the United States.

The region that is called the post-Soviet space has been a Russian preserve for a long time under the Czars and then the Soviet Union. For the Russians, the cultural, historical and linguistic linkages with the states in the post-Soviet space are significant. Even when the Soviet Union was dismantled, Russia expected the seceding republics to remain within its sphere of influence and set-up the Commonwealth of Independent States (CIS). However, the first decade following the collapse of the Soviet Union was one of painful transition for Russia. NATO steadily expanded eastward, in spite of assurances to the contrary given by George H.W. Bush, Margaret Thatcher and Helmut Kohl to Mikhail Gorbachev. Severe financial constraints left Russia rudderless and unable to respond to such challenges. As Dmitry Trenin argues, 'By 1999, when NATO wrested Kosovo from Belgrade, NATO had already enlarged with the additions of the Czech Republic, Hungary and Poland. Russia, for the first time in 250 years, had ceased to be a power in Europe. It was now simply the former Soviet Union, nothing more, nothing less.'[27] So as Putin took charge and Russia rebounded economically aided by high oil prices, it could afford to defend what it perceived to be its legitimate spheres of interest in its near abroad.

Russia was particularly concerned about Ukraine and Georgia as these two states were moving forward in pursuit of NATO membership. Russia's sense of insecurity was heightened by the fact that it is not really a part of the current security architecture of Europe.[28] Meanwhile, Russia was also alarmed by the democracy-promotion agenda of the George W. Bush administration and the 2003-2005 'colour revolutions' in Georgia, Ukraine, and Kyrgyzstan, which it saw as US geopolitical advances into the post-Soviet space.[29] For Russia, the Georgian War was not really about the rights of ethnic Russians or the future of Abkhazia and South Ossetia: it was Russia's assertion of its willingness to act forcefully in defending its interests in the post-Soviet space.

Presently, Ukraine appears relatively settled in Moscow's favour after the election of President Viktor Yanukovych. He has announced a non-bloc foreign policy, effectively reversing the course to pursue NATO membership. After Yanukovych took charge, Russia managed to get a 25-year extension of the lease to use Ukrainian naval bases for the Russian Black Sea Fleet by offering Ukraine natural gas at concessional rates. Such a move forecloses completely 'Ukraine's entry into NATO in the foreseeable future, since NATO members are not permitted to host non-NATO military bases within their borders'.[30] Meanwhile Yanukovych made it clear that Ukraine will not join the European missile defence system sponsored by NATO nor join the group itself.[31]

In Central Asia, things are further complicated by the growing presence of China, which is aggressively wooing the energy-rich republics. China shares borders with three Central Asian Republics and in the wake of the global financial recession, it has significantly increased its profile in the region, especially through investments, loans and Cross Border Pipelines, bypassing Russia. Because of Washington's overbearing attitude towards it, Russia is compelled to share with China an interest in limiting American influence in the region even as China's increasing engagement with Central Asia is happening at the expense of Russia. While Sino-Russian ties appear to be stable at the moment, China's seemingly inexorable rise can lead to serious problems in this relationship. However, as

Stephen Pifer says, it is not clear how 'Washington might be able to exploit this possible rupture to improve its own position – or whether it would be advisable to try'.[32]

The United States seems to ignore the fact that Russia has legitimate interests in the post-Soviet space. While it is not likely that there will be a meeting of minds on the subject, as President Obama says, the US should learn to balance its interests in the region as well as understand its limitations. For example, the US is an extra-regional power unlike Russia and therefore its attempts to pull countries away from Russia or to block legal Russian activities there are unlikely to succeed.[33] Also, American interests will be best served if it stays out of regional skirmishes where its stakes are insignificant. Most of the regional players are adept in playing one big power against the other to ensure their interests are protected and therefore the 'United States must recognise that its interests are not identical to those of Russia's neighbours and avoid becoming their instrument in dealing with Russia'.[34]

Syria, Afghanistan and Iran

While Afghanistan and Iran have been moderate success stories of the reset, the Arab Spring has created insurmountable problems in the Middle East. Tensions began with Libya, as the US and NATO troops stretched the limits of the UN resolution (Russia had abstained from voting) and went ahead with the campaign to unseat Muammar Gaddafi. Military action in Libya went further than what Russia had expected and it has consistently opposed the US line in handling the Syrian crisis. Russia has robust ties with Bashar al-Assad's Syria and it maintains a naval base in Syria. Russia along with China vetoed the UNSC resolution against Syria as it keeps the option to remove Assad, even by force. The veto has enraged the Americans. Susan Rice, the US ambassador to the United Nations was acerbic in her reaction: 'The international community must protect the Syrian people from this abhorrent brutality, but a couple of members of this council remain steadfast in their willingness to sell out the Syrian people and shield a craven tyrant.'[35] The run up to the vote was equally dramatic. To canvas support for the resolution, Secretary of State Hillary Clinton tried to call up her Russian counterpart, Sergei Lavrov, who was on a trip to Australia. Lavrov refused to take the call and finally dismissed American complaints as 'bad manners'.

Moscow believes it has a lot at stake in Syria. It has waived Syrian debt from the Soviet times; it expects lucrative arms orders and had signed a defence deal in 2010. Russia has sold Syria arms worth more than a billion dollars in the last decade, including fighter aircraft, anti-tank missiles and surface-to-air missiles. It has also agreed to construct a nuclear plant in Syria. Financial considerations apart, Moscow is loathe to see another regime change in the Middle East, blessed by the United States and its Western allies.

While Syria continues to be a sticking point, the reset with Russia has produced encouraging results for the United States in two major areas of interest – Afghanistan and Iran. The most notable gain in Afghanistan is an agreement signed with Russia on setting up the Northern Distribution Network (NDN), a series of commercially based logistical arrangements connecting Baltic and Caspian ports with Afghanistan via Russia, Central Asia and the Caucasus. The NDN has eased some pressure off the 2,000 kilometre-long Pakistan Ground Lines of Communication (PAKGLOC), the logistical lifeline of the international forces in Afghanistan. The recent fallout between the US and Pakistan after the assassination of Osama bin Laden and the hardening of

Source: Stratfor

positions against each other in both countries has underscored the fragility of US-Pakistan relations. With the American troop reduction in Afghanistan, the importance of NDN will steadily increase. The NDN permits 4,300 US flights annually to Afghanistan (free of transit fees) and so far 150,000 US personnel and troops have transited via Russia. The route accounts for 45 percent of sustainment cargo moving into Afghanistan.

While the NDN has been a remarkable achievement for the United States, the future of Afghanistan still remains unclear. The commitment of 100,000 troops at a cost of $110 billion a year has become increasingly unpopular in the United States. Osama bin Laden's death has produced a clamour in Congress and among the public to proceed swiftly with the drawdown. President Obama had announced that the United States would withdraw 33,000 troops from Afghanistan by September 2012. Russia is wary about the drawdown and the proposed withdrawal even as it opposes permanent US bases in Afghanistan. Russian concerns are about the likelihood of Afghanistan relapsing into chaos and the Taliban recapturing power yet again. Unlike the United States, Afghanistan is in Russia's extended neighbourhood and instability there can quickly spill over into Central Asia. The restive southern Caucasus with a considerable Muslim population adds to Russia's worry. It is already negotiating with Tajikistan to place its soldiers again in the Afghan-Tajik border region. The threat of narcotics traffic is another major cause of worry for Russia.

Russian thinking on the future of Afghanistan can be summed up from the Valdai discussion Club's 2011 report on the US-Russia relations: 'Since the United States and NATO are unable to stabilise the situation in Afghanistan through a victory over the Taliban or an agreement with it on stable terms that would be acceptable to the Coalition, Afghanistan will continue to be a source of regional instability, international terrorism, and religious extremism. As early as within the next few years, Russia may face the threat of a new regional war in Tajikistan as a result of the export of instability from Afghanistan – especially as internal sources of instability are exacerbating in Central Asia.'[36] Considering the historical, political and strategic linkages and vital stakes Russia has with Afghanistan, Moscow expects the United States to take it into confidence in major policy decisions regarding Afghanistan.

The Contributors

C. Raja Mohan is a Distinguished Fellow at the ORF and leads the Strategic Studies Initiative of the Foundation. He is also a foreign affairs columnist for *The Indian Express*, a Visiting Research Professor at the Institute of South Asian Studies, Singapore, and a Non-Resident Senior Associate at the Carnegie Endowment for International Peace, Washington D.C. He is currently a member of India's National Security Advisory Board and has also served there earlier during 1998–2000 and 2004–06. His books include, *Crossing the Rubicon: The Shaping of India's New Foreign Policy* (2004), *Impossible Allies: Nuclear India, United States and the Global Order* (2006) and *Samudra Manthan: Sino-Indian Rivalry in the Indo-Pacific* (2012).

Saeed Naqvi is a senior journalist and writer. In pursuit of his vision that India must cover foreign affairs, Saeed has travelled to over 100 countries and interviewed a wide range of world leaders. His articles appear in various newspapers in India and abroad. He has authored books and lectured in Indian and foreign universities.

A leading Indian scholar in the field of Japanese Studies, ***K.V. Kesavan*** is currently a Distinguished Fellow at Observer Research Foundation, New Delhi. He is in charge of the Japanese Studies programme at ORF. He was Professor of Japanese Studies on the faculty of the Centre for East Asian Studies, School of International Studies, Jawaharlal Nehru University, New Delhi, for over 30 years. Author of several books on Japan, he has also written numerous research papers in Indian and foreign academic journals on Japan's foreign policy and domestic politics. He has been a Visiting Professor/Fellow at several universities in Japan and the US. In 2001, he received the Japanese Foreign Minister's Commendation Award for his contribution to closer understanding between India and Japan.

K.Yhome is a Research Fellow at the ORF. He completed his Ph.D. from JNU. His research interests include India's neighbourhood, Southeast Asia and China's Southwest Provinces. He has published a book, *Myanmar: Can the Generals Resist Change?*, and contributed chapters and articles in edited books and journals.

Angira Sen Sarma is a Research Fellow at Indian Council of World Affairs (ICWA), New Delhi. Her research interests include Central Asia, mainly focussing on India-Central Asia relations, foreign policy of the five Central Asian Republics, security issues and regional organisations. She has authored a book – *India and Central Asia: Redefining Energy and Trade Links* – and has also contributed chapters in edited books. Before joining ICWA, she worked with the ORF. She completed her Ph.D. and M.Phil from JNU.

Ajish P. Joy is assistant editor, *The Week*. Prior to this, he worked with the ORF. He completed his Ph.D. from the School of International Studies, JNU. He has authored a book: *India, Central Asia and Russia: Potential for Regional Cooperation*. He has also contributed chapters and articles in edited books and journals.

Uma Purushothaman is an Associate Fellow at the ORF. She has a Ph.D. from JNU. She has written several articles on US foreign policy, particularly focussing on different aspects of Indo-US relations. Her areas of interest include US foreign and domestic policies, China-Russia relations, Indian foreign policy, human security, food security, foreign aid and soft power.

Notes

Chapter 1

1. See Eric Johnson, 'The Future of US-Japan Relations in a McCain or Obama Presidency : Does Japan Matter?' *Japan Times*, 1 November 2008.
2. 'Japan Info Japan: A Cornerstone of US Foreign Policy,' http://www.usent-japan.go.jp (en/c/2009/japaninfo0902.html)
3. 'Clinton in Tokyo,' http://www-washington.con/wp-ohjn/content/article/2009/02/11/AR2009021600829/html)
4. 'US Secretary of State Pledges Support for Japan on Abduction Issue,' http://www.news.inhuenot/con/english/2009.2-17/content 10835546.hto
5. 'Clinton Confronts Japan's Abduction Issue,' *Asia Times*, www.A Times.com www.atyimes/a times/Japan/KB19dh0/html
6. See Tobias Harris, 'Gates Rules out Renegotiation of Okinawa Deal with Japan', *East Asia Forum*, www-eastasia forum.org2000/10/24.
7. See the Joint Statement Policy Speech by PM Naoto Kan at the 174th Session of the Diet. http://www.kantei.go.jp/foreign/kan/statement/201006/11syosin_e.html

8. See Obama's Speech in the New York Times, http://www.nytimes.com/2011/03/17/us/politics/18obama-japan-text.html
9. Remarks by President Obama and Prime Minister Kan Naoto of Japan before Bilateral Meeting in Deauville, France; *The Outline of Japan-US Summit Meeting*, 22 June 2011, http://www.mofa.go.jp/announce/jfpu/2011/6/0622.html
10. See Michael Green and Nicholas Szechenyi, 'US-Japan Relations: Kicking the Kan down in the Road,' *Comparative Connections – A Triannual E-Journal on East Asian Bilateral Relations*, September 2011.
11. See the Preamble of the Joint Statement of the US-Japan Security Consultative Committee issued on 21 June 2011, (US Department of State, Washington DC).
12. *Ibid.*
13. *Ibid.*
14. *Daily Yomiuri*, 24 August 2011.
15. *Daily Yomiuri*, 23 September 2011.
16. See Douglas H. Paal, 'Obama in Asia: Policy and Politics,' *Asia Pacific Brief* (Carnegie Endowment, Washington DC), 6 December 2011.
17. See Visit to Myanmar by Koichiro Gemba, Minister for Foreign Affairs of Japan (summary), www.mofa.go.jp/region/asia-paci/myanmar/meeting112.html
18. Joint Vision for the Alliance of the United States of America and the Republic of Korea, http://www.cfr.org/proliferation/joint-vision-allianceunited-states-america-republic-kore
19. See *East Asian Strategic Review 2011*, (The National Institute for Defence Studies, Japan), p. 233.
20. See 'North Korea's Belligerent Bombing of South Rebuked,' http://www.bloomberg.com.news/2010-11-23.north-korea-attack-on.southern-island-dr
21. *Ibid.*
22. See Abraham M. Denmark, 'Crowded Waters,' 7 June 2011, *Foreign Policy*, http://www.foreignp olicy.com/articles/2011/06/07/crowded_

waters?page=full

23. See Gerald Curtis,'Charting a Future Course for US-Japan Relations,' in *Asia-Pacific Review, (IIPS, Tokyo),* Vol. 18, no. 1, 2011, pp. 3–4.
24. *Ibid.*, p. 4.

Chapter 2

1. 'Sustaining US Global Leadership: Priorities for 21st Century Defence,' Department of Defense, 3 January 2012, http://www.defence.gov/news/defence_Strategic_Guidance.pdf p. 2.
2. http://www.census.gov/foreign-trade/balance/c5700.html
3. Wayne M. Morrison, 'China-US Trade Issues,' 7 January 2011, CRS Report, p. 1.
4. http://www.census.gov/foreign-trade/balance/c5700.html
5. Susan V. Lawrence and Thomas Lum, 'US-China Relations: Policy Issues,' CRS Report for Congress, 12 January 2011, http://assets.opencrs.com/rpts/R41108_20110112.pdf 2011, p. 11.
6. Keith B. Richburg, 'US Pivot to Asia makes China Nervous,' 16 November 2011, http://www.washingtonpost.com/world/asia_pacific/us-pivot-to-asia-makes-china-nervous/2011/11/15/gIQAsQpVRN_story.html
7. Susan V. Lawrence and Thomas Lum, 'US-China Relations: Policy Issues,' CRS Report for Congress, 12 January 2011, http://assets.opencrs.com/rpts/R41108_20110112.pdf, p.1.
8. Ben Baden, 'Why China Has a Point About Quantitative Easing,' October 29, 2010, http://money.usnews.com/money/business-economy/articles/2010/10/29/why-china-has-a-point-about-quantitative-easing
9. Susan V. Lawrence and Thomas Lum, 'US-China Relations: Policy Issues,' CRS Report for Congress, 12 January 2011, http://assets.opencrs.com/rpts/R41108_20110112.pdf, p. 26.
10. Tetsuo Kotani, 'Why China Wants the South China Sea,' 18 July 2011, *The Diplomat*, http://the-diplomat.com/2011/07/18/why-

china-wants-the-south-china-sea/

11. Susan V. Lawrence and Thomas Lum, 'US-China Relations: Policy Issues,' CRS Report for Congress, 12 January 2011, http://assets.opencrs.com/rpts/R41108_20110112.pdf, p. 27.
12. Remarks at Press Availability, Hillary Rodham Clinton, Secretary of State, National Convention Center, Hanoi, Vietnam, July 23, 2010, http://www.state.gov/secretary/rm/2010/07/145095.htm
13. Statement of Admiral Robert F. Willard, US Navy Commander, US Pacific Command before the Senate Armed Services Committee on US Pacific Command Posture, 12 April 2011, http://armed-services.senate.gov/statemnt/2011/04%20April/Willard%2004-12-11pdf, p.10
14. Chengxin Pan, 'Is the South China Sea a New "Dangerous Ground" for US-China Rivalry?', 24 May 2011, http://www.eastasiaforum.org/2011/05/24/is-the-south-china-sea-a-new-dangerous-ground-for-us-china-rivalry/
15. Austin Ramzy and Dalian, 'Troubled Waters: Why China's Navy Makes Asia Nervous,' *TIME*, 10 August 2011, http://www.time.com/time/world/article/0,8599,2087973,00.html#ixzz1nfa72G1X
16. Susan V. Lawrence and Thomas Lum, 'US-China Relations: Policy Issues,' CRS Report for Congress, 12 January 2011, http://assets.opencrs.com/rpts/R41108_20110112.pdf, p. 28.
17. Tetsuo Kotani, 'Why China Wants the South China Sea,' 18 July 2011, *The Diplomat*, http://the-diplomat.com/2011/07/18/why-china-wants-the-south-china-sea/
18. Susan V. Lawrence and Thomas Lum, 'US-China Relations: Policy Issues,' *CRS Report for Congress*, 12 January 2011, http://assets.opencrs.com/rpts/R41108_20110112.pdf, p. 28.
19. For more details, see http://www.state.gov/documents/organization/160451.pdf, 8 April 2011.
20. For more details, see 'Full Text of Human Rights Record of the United States in 2010,' http://news.xinhuanet.com/english2010/china/2011-04/10/c_13822287.htm

21. Susan V. Lawrence and Thomas Lum, 'US-China Relations: Policy Issues,' *CRS Report for Congress*, 12 January 2011, http://assets.opencrs.com/rpts/R41108_20110112.pdf, p. 22.
22. Quoted in Susan V. Lawrence and Thomas Lum, 'US-China Relations: Policy Issues,' *CRS Report for Congress*, 12 January 2011, http://assets.opencrs.com/rpts/R41108_20110112.pdf, p. 23.
23. John W. Garver, 'Is China Playing a Dual Game in Iran?', *The Washington Quarterly*, Winter 2011, p. 79, pp. 75–88.
24. Susan V. Lawrence and Thomas Lum, 'US-China Relations: Policy Issues,' *CRS Report for Congress*, 12 January 2011, http://assets.opencrs.com/rpts/R41108_20110112.pdf p. 24.
25. Austin Ramzy and Dalian, 'Troubled Waters: Why China's Navy Makes Asia Nervous,' *TIME*, 10 August 2011.
26. Statement of Admiral Robert F. Willard, US Navy Commander, US Pacific Command before the Senate Armed Services Committee on US Pacific Command Posture, 12 April 2011, http://armed-services.senate.gov/statemnt/2011/04%20April/Willard%2004-12-11.pdf, p. 10.
27. Report to Congress, 'US-China Economic and Security Review Commission,' November 2011, http://www.uscc.gov/annual_report/2011/annual_report_full_11.pdf, p. 18.
28. Quadrennial defence Review Report, Department of Defense, February 2010, http://www.defence.gov/qdr/images/QDR_as_of_12Feb10_1000.pdf, p. 31.
29. 'China's Growing Role in Africa: Implications for US Policy,' Testimony by David H. Shin, 1 November 2011, Hearing Held by the Senate Committee on Foreign Relations Subcommittee on African Affairs, http://www.foreign.senate.gov/imo/media/doc/David_Shinn_Testimony.pdf, pp. 2–3.
30. Katherine Koleski, 'China in Latin America,' US-China Economic and Security Review Commission, 27 May 2011, http://www.uscc.gov/Backgrounder_China_in_Latin_America.pdf, p. 17.
31. Katherine Koleski, 'China in Latin America,' US-China Economic

and Security Review Commission, 27 May 2011, http://www.uscc.gov/Backgrounder_China_in_Latin_America.pdf, p. 17.

32. 'Country Reports on Terrorism 2010,' August 2011, http://www.state.gov/documents/organization/170479.pdf, p. 34.

Chapter 3

1. David Capie and Amitav Acharya, 'The United States and the East Asia Summit: A New Beginning?', *East Asia Forum*, 20 November 2011, http://www.eastasiaforum.org/2011/11/20/the-united-states-and-the-east-asia-summit-a-new-beginning/
2. Hillary Clinton, 'America's Pacific Century,' *Foreign Policy*, November 2011.
3. See S. R. Joey Long, 'The United States, Southeast Asia, and Asia-Pacific Security,' in *US Re-engagement in Asia, Asia Policy* 12 (July 2011), http://www.nbr.org/publications/asia_policy/Preview/AP12_B_EngageRT_preview.pdf
4. See Evelyn Goh, 'Southeast Asia: Strategic Diversification in the "Asian Century",' in Ashley Tellis, Mercy Kuo, and Andrew Marble (eds), *Strategic Asia 2008-09: Challenges and Choices* (Washington DC: The National Bureau of Asian Research, 2008), pp. 261–96.
5. Clifford McCoy, 'US Southeast Asia Pose Risks China Clash,' *Asia Times Online*, 1 September 2010, at http://www.atimes.com/atimes/Southeast_Asia/LI01Ae01.html
6. The United States assistance to Indonesian Special Force or the Kopassus was banned for the involvement in human rights abuses in Aceh, East Timor, Papua and during riots in Jakarta in 1998.
7. Clifford McCoy, 'US Southeast Asia pose risks China clash', *Asia Times Online*, 1 September 2010, at http://www.atimes.com/atimes/Southeast_Asia/LI01Ae01.html
8. The TPP is a multilateral free trade agreement involving nine countries – Australia, Brunei, Chile, Malaysia, New Zealand, Peru, Singapore, the United States and Vietnam. It is expected to lead

to an Asia-Pacific Free Trade Agreement (FTAAP).

9. Progress on trade issues has been made in the past rounds of negotiations, but work there still needs to be done on intellectual property rights, e-commerce and environmental issues.
10. See Catharin Dalpino, 'The United States-Thailand Alliance: Issues for a New Dialogue,' *The National Bureau of Asian Research, NBR Special Report #33*, October 2011.
11. Robert Scher, Deputy Assistant Secretary of Defence, 'China's Activities in Southeast Asia and the Implications for US Interests,' statement before the US-China Economic and Security Review Commission,' Washington DC, 4 February 2010, http://www.uscc.gov/hearings/2010hearings/transcripts/10_02_04_trans/10_02_04_trans.pdf
12. See Sebastian Strangio, 'US cables chart China's rise in Cambodia,' *Asia Times Online*, 20 July 2011.
13. Daniel Kliman and Abraham M Denmark, 'How to Get Southeast Asia Right,' *The Diplomat*, 2 February 2011.
14. Ray Hervandi, 'US-Southeast Asia Trade Triples Over Last Two Decades,' *ASEAN Matters for America*, 24 May 2011.
15. 'Senator calls for US-ASEAN free trade agreement,' *Taipei Times*, 11 October 2009, http://www.taipeitimes.com/News/biz/archives/2009/10/11/2003455712
16. 'Lugar urges US-Asean FTA negotiations,' *The Nation*, 29 June 2011, http://www.nationmultimedia.com/home/Lugar-urges-US-Asean-FTA-negotiations-30158977.html
17. Robert Scher, Deputy Assistant Secretary of Defence, 'China's Activities in Southeast Asia and the Implications for US Interests,' statement before the US-China Economic and Security Review Commission', Washington DC, 4 February 2010, http://www.uscc.gov/hearings/2010hearings/transcripts/10_02_04_trans/10_02_04_trans.pdf
18. 'China's direct investment to ASEAN countries reaches $2.57b,'

China Daily, 15 July 2011, http://www.chinadaily.com.cn/business/2011-03/02/content_12104984.htm

19. Chengyin Pan,'Is the South China Sea a New "Dangerous Ground" for US-China Rivalry,' *East Asia Forum*, 24 May 2011, http://www.eastasiaforum.org/2011/05/24/is-the-south-china-sea-a-new-dangerous-ground-for-us-china-rivalry/
20. Richard P. Cronin, 'China's Activities in Southeast Asia and the Implications for US Interests,' Statement before the US-China Economic and Security Review Commission, Washington DC, 4 February 2010, http://www.uscc.gov/hearings/2010hearings/transcripts/10_02_04_trans/10_02_04_trans.pdf
21. Richard P. Cronin, 'China's Activities in Southeast Asia and the Implications for US Interests', Statement before the US-China Economic and Security Review Commission, Washington DC, 4 February 2010, http://www.uscc.gov/hearings/2010hearings/transcripts/10_02_04_trans/10_02_04_trans.pdf
22. Chengyin Pan, 'Is the South China Sea a New "Dangerous Ground"for US-China Rivalry,' *East Asia Forum*, 24 May 2011.
23. Representative Dana Rohrabacher, Statement to the US-China Economic and Security Review Commission, Washington DC, 4 February 2010, http://www.uscc.gov/hearings/2010hearings/transcripts/10_02_04_trans/10_02_04_trans.pdf
24. Ernest Z. Bower, 'Hillary Clinton's Asia Sojourn,' 19 July 2011, Center for Strategic and International Studies.
25. See Carlyle A. Thayer , 'The Rise of China and India: Challenging or Reinforcing Southeast Asia's Autonomy?', in Ashley J. Tellis, Travis Tanner, and Jessica Keough, (eds), 'Asia Responds to its Rising Powers: China and India', *Strategic Asia 2011–12*, The National Bureau of Asian Research, 2011.

Chapter 4

1. For a discussion, see Ashley Tellis, 'The Merits of De-Hyphenation.

Explaining US Success in Engaging India and Pakistan,' *Washington Quarterly*, Vol. 31, No. 4, Autumn 2008, pp. 21–42.

2. For his first articulation on foreign policy at the start of the campaign for the 2008 presidential elections see, Barack Obama, 'Renewing American Leadership,' *Foreign Affairs*, July–August 2007.
3. Andrew Whitehead, 'Obama's Kashmir Conundrum,' *BBC* World Service News, 21 January 2009, http://news.bbc.co.uk/2/hi/south_asia/7838440.stm
4. Lawrence Wright, 'The Double Game,' *New Yorker*, 16 May 2011, http://www.newyorker.com/reporting/2011/05/16/110516fa_fact_wright; see also Colin Cookman, Brian Katulis, and Caroline Wadhams, 'The Limits of US Assistance to Pakistan' (Washington DC: Center for American Progress, July 2011).
5. Katelyn Sabochik, 'President Obama on the way forward in Afghanistan,' The White House Blog, 22 June 2011, http://www.whitehouse.gov/blog/2011/06/22/president-obama-way-forward-afghanistan
6. Mathew Rosenberg, 'Karzai Told to Dump US: Pakistan Urges Afghanistan to Ally with Islamabad, Beijing,' *Wall Street Journal*, 27 April 2011.
7. For a discussion, see Daniel Twining, 'America's Grand Design in Asia,' *Washington Quarterly*, Vol. 30, No. 3, Summer 2007, pp. 79–94
8. Zbigniew Brzezinski, 'The Group of Two that Could Change the World', *Financial Times* (London), 13 January 2009.
9. 'US-China Joint Statement,' Beijing, 17 November 2009, http://beijing.usembassy-china.org.cn/111709.html
10. See Obama's remarks welcoming PM Singh at the White House, 24 November 2009, http://www.whitehouse.gov/the-press-office/remarks-president-obama-and-prime-minister-singh-india-during-arrival-ceremony
11. 'Joint Statement of Prime Minister Manmohan Singh and President Barack Obama,' New Delhi, November 8, 2010, http://www.mea.gov.in/mystart.php?id=530516632

12. Hillary Clinton, 'Remarks on India and the United States: A Vision for 21st Century,' Chennai, 20 July 2011, http://www.state.gov/secretary/rm/2011/07/168840.htm
13. 'Hillary Curzon', editorial in *Business Standard* (New Delhi), 26 July 2011, http://www.business-standard.com/india/news/hillary-curzon/443825/
14. Clinton Speech in Chennai, op. cit., n. (13).
15. *Ibid.*
16. See for example, Michael Auslin, *Indo-Pacific Commons: Towards a Regional Strategy* (Washington DC: American Enterprise Institute, 2010).

Chapter 6

1. *BP Statistical Review of World Energy*, June 2011, bp.com/statisticalreview
2. Ambassador Chas W. Freeman, Jr., 'American Foreign Policy and the Arab World,' Speech delivered to the Summer Institute of the Washington World Affairs Council, 25 June 2007.
3. US Energy Information Administration, 'US Imports by Country of Origin: Petroleum and Other Liquids,' http://www.eia.doe.gov/dnav/pet/pet_move_impcus_a2_nus_ep00_im0_mbbl_a.htm
4. Milton R. Copulos, 'The Real Cost of Imported Oil,' *Washington Times*, 23 July 2003. p. A17, quoted in Geoffrey Kemp and Paul Saunders, *America, Russia, and the Greater Middle East: Challenges and Opportunities*, The Nixon Center, Washington D.C., 2003, p. 8.
5. Walter Russell Mead, 'Why We're in the Gulf,' 27 December 2007, *Wall Street Journal*, http://www.cfr.org/energy-security/why-were-gulf/p15139
6. *Ibid.*
7. Nader Habibi and Eckart Woertz, 'US-Arab Economic Relations and the Obama Administration,' February 2009, http://www.brandeis.edu/crown/publications/meb/MEB34.pdf, p. 2
8. Leon Hadar, *Sandstorm: Policy Failure in the Middle East*, (New York:

Palgrave Macmillan), 2005, p. 5.

9. Press conference with President Carter, 12 May 1977, http://www.mfa.gov.il/MFA/Foreign%20Relations/Israels%20Foreign%20Relations%20since%201947/1974-1977/211%20Press%20conference%20with%20President%20Carter-%2012%20May
10. Leon Hadar, *Sandstorm: Policy Failure in the Middle East* (New York: Palgrave Macmillan), 2005, p.17.
11. *Ibid.*, p.12.
12. Helena Cobban, 'US Policy and Egypt after Mubarak's Resignation,' http://thehill.com/blogs/congress-blog/foreign-policy/143839-us-policy-and-egypt-after-mubaraks-resignation-
13. Ana Echague, 'Change or Continuity? US Policy towards the Middle East and its Implications for EU Policy', *Working Paper* no. 95, March 2010, p.1.
14. *Ibid.*
15. 'Key Political Risks to Watch Out in Bahrain,' http://us.mobile.reuters.com/article/topNews/idUSTRE71 G5XX20110217
16. Brad Knickerbocker, 'US Faces Difficult Situation in Bahrain, Home to US Fifth Fleet,' 19 February 2011, http://www.csmonitor.com/USA/Foreign-Policy/2011/0219/US-faces-difficult-situationin-Bahrain-home-to-US-Fifth-Fleet
17. Christopher M. Blanchard and Paul K. Kerr, 'The United Arab Emirates Nuclear Program and Proposed US Nuclear Cooperation,' 20 December 2010, *CRS Report*, http://fpc.state.gov/documents/organization/154163.pdf, p.1.
18. Senate Committee on Banking, Housing and Urban Development, Testimony of James B. Steinberg, Deputy Secretary of State, 6 October 2009.
19. Neil Patrick, 'The Gulf States and a fourth Gulf War,' Royal United Services Institute, http://www.rusi.org/analysis/commentary/ref:C4A9E4172ED746/
20. Ana Echague, 'Change or Continuity? US Policy towards the Middle East and its Implications for EU Policy,' *Working Paper* no.95, March

2010, http://www.fride.org/publication/747/us-policy-towards-the-middle-east-and-its-implications-for-eu-policy, p. 2.

21. Joby Warrick, 'US Steps Up Arms Sales to Persian Gulf Allies,' 31 January 2010, *Washington Post.*
22. Press Briefing, R. Nicholas Burns, Under Secretary of State for Political Affairs, 'US Aid and Military Support to the Middle East Region,' 30 July 2007, http://merln.ndu.edu/archivepdf/NEA/State/89807.pdf
23. Nader Habibi and Eckart Woertz, 'US-Arab Economic Relations and the Obama Administration,' February 2009, http://www.brandeis.edu/crown/publications/meb/MEB34.pdf, p. 5.
24. http://www.ustr.gov/countries-regions/europe-middle-east/middle-east/north-africa
25. *Ibid.*
26. Richard F. Grimmett, 'Conventional Arms Transfers to Developing Nations, 2002–2009,' 10 September 2010, *CRS Report*, p. 47.
27. *Ibid.*, p. 46.
28. Christina Lin, 'The New Silk Road: China's Energy Strategy in the Greater Middle East,' Policy Focus no. 109, April 2011, The Washington Institute for Near East Policy, http://www.washingtoninstitute.org/pubPDFs/PolicyFocus109.pdf, p. x
29. Ian Lesser, (undated), 'Rediscovering the Mediterranean: A Transatlantic Perspective on Security and Strategy,' *Policy Brief*, German Marshall Fund of the US, p. 4.
30. For more details, see 'China's Missile Exports and Assistance to the Middle East,' http://www.nti.org/db/china/mmepos.htm; also see, 'The Proliferation of Weapons of Mass Destruction in the Mediterranean,' http://www.ieei.pt/publicacoes/artigo.php?artigo=142
31. Michael Singh and Jacqueline Newmyer Deal, *Foreign Policy*, 31 October 2011, http://www.foreignpolicy.com/articles/2011/10/31/china_iran_nuclear_relationship?page=full
32. Michael Singh and Jacqueline Newmyer Deal, op. cit.
33. 'Sustaining US Global Leadership: Priorities for 21st Century

Defence,' Department of Defence, 3 January 2012, http://www.defence.gov/news/ defence_Strategic_Guidance.pdf, p. 2.

34. This speech can be accessed at http://www.whitehouse.gov/the-press-office/2011/05/19/remarks-president-middle-east-and-north-africa

Chapter 7

1. Charles William Maynes, 'America Discovers Central Asia,' *Foreign Affairs*, March/April, 2003 Vol. 82, no. 2, p. 121.
2. Elizabeth Wishnick, *Growing US Security Interests in Central Asia*, Strategic Studies Institute, United States Army War College, 2005
3. Speech by Ambassador A Elizabeth Jones, Assistant Secretary of State for European and Eurasian Affairs as prepared for delivery at the German Studies Association Annual Conference, *September 11, 2001: Attack on America*, 5 October 2001, http://avalon.law.yale.edu/sept11/jones_001.asp
4. Martha Brill Olcott, *Central Asia's Second Chance*, Washington, DC: Carnegie Endowment for International Peace, 2005, p. 2.
5. Andrew C Kuchin, *et.al*, 'The Northern Distribution Network and Afghanistan: Geopolitical Challenges and Opportunities. A Report of the CSIS Transnational Threats Project and the Russia and Eurasia Program,' January, Washington, DC: Center for Strategic & International Studies (CSIS), 2010, http://csis.org/files/publication/091229_Kuchins_NDNandAfghan_Web.pdf
6. Robert O. Blake, Jr. (2011), Testimony before the House Foreign Affairs Committee, Subcommittee on Europe and Eurasia, March 10, 2011, http://ww.state.gov/p/sca/rls/rmks/2011/158199.htm
7. Vassilis K. Fouskas, *Zones of Conflict: US Foreign Policy in the Balkans and the Greater Middle East,* London, Sterling, Virginia: Pluto Press, 2003, p. 12.
8. *Ibid.*, p. 19.
9. *Ibid.*

10. Kenley Butler, 'Weapons of Mass Destruction in Central Asia,' James Martin Centre for Non Proliferation Studies (CNS) Monterey Institute of International Studies, *NTI Issue Brief*, October 2002, http://www.nti.org/e_research/e3_19a.html
11. Togzhan Kassenova (2007), 'Central Asia: Regional security and WMD Proliferation Threats,' http://www.unidiv.org/pdf/articles/pdf-art2684.pdf
12. *Ibid.*
13. Office of the Coordinator of US Assistance to Europe and Eurasia (2002–2008), 'US Government Assistance to and Cooperative Activities with Eurasia,' *Annual Reports*, www.state.gov/p/eur/ace.
14. Address by President Nazarbayev, 'Kazakhstan Stands on the Threshold of Major Breakthrough in Development,' http://prosites-kazakhembus.homestead.com/echo24.html
15. Remarks by US Energy Deputy Secretary Daniel Poneman at the Kazakhstan International Oil and Gas Exhibition and Conference, 7 October 2009, Almaty, Kazakhstan, http://kazakhstan.usembassy.gov/tr-10-07-09.html
16. US Department of State, 'Background Note: Kazakhstan,' 20 April 2009, http://www.state.gov/r/pa/ei/bgn/5487.htm
17. Daniel Poneman, op. cit., n. (15).
18. Background Note: Kazakhstan, op. cit., n. (16).
19. US Census Bureau, Foreign Trade, http://www.census.gov/foreign-trade/balance/c4634.html
20. Kenley Butler, op. cit., n. (10).
21. *Ibid.*
22. Background Note: Kazakhstan op. cit., n. (16).
23. J.D. Crouch II, 'Defence and Security Cooperation in Central Asia,' Subcommittee Central Asia and the South Caucasus Committee on Foreign Relations, US Senate, 27 June 2002, www.dod.gov/dodgc/olc/docs/test02-06-27Crouch.rtf
24. John C.K. Daly, 'Chronology of US-Uzbekistan Relations, 2001–2005' in John C.K. Daly, et. al, *Anatomy of a Crisis: US-Uzbekistan*

Relations, 2001-2005, February 2006, *Silk Road Paper*, Central Asia-Caucasus Institute & Silk Road Studies Program, The Jamestown Foundation and United States Institute of Peace, p. 71, http://www.silkroadstudies.org/new/inside/publications/0602Uzbek.pdf

25. (A) Office of the Coordinator of US Assistance to the NIS, 'FY 1995–US Government Assistance to and Cooperative Activities with the New Independent States of the Former Soviet Union,' www.state.gov/www/regions/nis/nis_assist_inde.html. and (B)Bureau of European and Eurasian Affairs, 'US Government Assistance to and Cooperative Activities with Eurasia-FY 2002,' http://www.state.gov/p/eur/rls/rpt/c10250.htm
26. ICG Report, International Crisis Group Report, 'Central Asia's Energy Risks,' *Asia Report No. 133, 24*, May 2007, p. 16, http://www.crisisgroup.org/~/media/Files/asia/central asia/133_central_asia_s_energy_risks.ashx
27. Ministry of Foreign Affairs of the Republic of Uzbekistan, 'The Uzbek-American cooperation,' http://www.mfa.uz/modules.php?op=modload&name=Sections&
28. *Ibid.*
29. US Department of State, 'Background Note: Uzbekistan,' Bureau of South and Central Asian Affairs, http://www.state.gov/r/pa/ei/bgn/2924.htm
30. US Department of State, Background Note: Kyrgyzstan, Bureau of South and Central Asian Affairs http://www.state.gov/r/pa/ei/bgn/5755.htm
31. NATO's Relations with the Kyrgyz Republic, http://www.nato.int/issues/nato-kyrgyzstan/
32. (A) Office of the Coordinator of US Assistance to the NIS, 'FY 1995–US Government Assistance to and Cooperative Activities with the New Independent States of the Former Soviet Union,' www.state.gov/www/regions/nis/nis_assist_inde.html. and (B)Bureau of European and Eurasian Affairs, 'US Government Assistance to and Cooperative Activities with Eurasia–FY 2002,' [Online: Web]

Accessed 12 February 2010, URL: http://www.state.gov/p/eur/rls/rpt/c10250.htm

33. 'Manas Air Base (Transit Center at Manas, Kyrgyzstan),' http://topics.nytimes.com/top/reference/timestopics/subjects/t/transit_center_at_manas_kyrgyzstan/index.html
34. Kyrgyz Government Urges US to Suspend Fuel Deal,' 5 November 2010, http://www.rferl.org/content/Kyrgyz_Government_Urges_US_To_Suspend_Fuel_Deal/2212244.html
35. 'Kyrgyzstan, US sign new Manas base fuel deal after criticism of supplier,' 9 February 2011 http://english.peopledaily.com.cn/90001/90777/90851/7282433.html
36. *Ibid.*
37. K. Kumkova, 'Kyrgyzstan: Another Rent Showdown for Manas Base?' 3 April 2012 http://www.eursianet.org/node/65218
38. Joshua Kucera, 'Kyrgyzstan Open to Extending Manas Lease, Getting US Drones,' 3 April 2012, http://www.eurasianet.org/node/65215
39. *Ibid.*
40. Eric Marat, 'Kyrgyz defence Ministry Agrees to Host US Base Beyond 2014,' 3 April 2012, http://www.jamestown.org/single/?no_cache=1&tx_ttnews%5Btt_news%5D39222
41. CSTO Summit Held in Moscow, 21 December 2011 http://www.itar-tass.com/en/c142/302819.html
42. Jim Nichol, 'Tajikistan: Recent Development and US Interests,' Congressional Research Service, *CRS Report for Congress*, 10 February 2011, p.1., http://www.fas.org/sgp/crs/row/98-594.pdf
43. US Department of State, FY 2010 Congressional Budget Justification for Foreign Operations, 'Tajikistan: Foreign Assistance Program Overview,' http://www.state.gov/documents/organization/124072.pdf
44. Jim Nichol, op. cit., n. (42), p. 2.
45. *Ibid.*, p. 3.
46. *Ibid.*
47. 'US Military Commander Discusses Security Cooperation with Tajik President,' March 2012, http://www.rferl.org/

articleprintview/24533469.html

48. *Ibid.*
49. US Department of State, Bureau of South and Central Asian Affairs, 'Background Note: Tajikistan,' http://www.state.gov/r/pa/ei/bgn/5775.htm
50. Jim Nichol, op. cit., n. (42), p. 2.
51. Background Note: Tajikistan, op. cit., n. (49).
52. *Ibid.*
53. US Department of State, Bureau of South and Central Asian Affairs, 'Background Note: Turkmenistan,' http://www.state.gov/r/pa/ei/bgn/35884.htm
54. Stephen J Blank, 'Turkmenistan and Central Asia After Niyazov,' Strategic Studies Institute, September 2007, [Online: Web] Accessed 11 October 2011, URL: http://www.strategicstudiesinstitute.army.mil/pdffiles/pub791.pdf
55. Turkmenistan-US Relations, Ashgabat, Turkmenistan, 16 April 2009, http://turkmenistan.usembassy.gov/transcript20090416.html.
56. Murat Laumulin, 'The Geopolitics of XXI Century in Central Asia,' The Kazakhstan Institute for Strategic Studies, Almaty, p. 65.
57. Marlene Laruelle and Sebastien Peyrouse, 'The United States in Central Asia; Reassessing a Challenging Partnership,' *Strategic Analysis*, Vol. 35, Issue 3, 2011, p. 430.

Chapter 8

1. Dmitry Trenin, 'Thinking Strategically about Russia,' Carnegie Moscow Centre, December 2008, http://www.carnegieendowment.org/files/thinking_strategically_russia.pdf
2. Stephen F. Cohen, 'Obama's Russia "Reset": Another Lost Opportunity?', *The Nation*, 20 June 2011, http://www.thenation.com/article/161063/obamas-russia-reset-another-lost-opportunity
3. Caroline Wyatt, 'Bush and Putin: Best of Friends,' *BBC News*, 16 June 2001, http://news.bbc.co.uk/2/hi/1392791.stm

4. US-Russian Bilateral Presidential Commission: Mission Statement, US Department of State. Available on http://www.state.gov/p/eur/ci/rs/usrussiabilat/c38418.htm
5. Joseph R. Biden Jr., 'The Next Steps in the US-Russia Reset,' *The New York Times*, 13 March 2011.
6. 'Russia Profile Weekly Experts Panel: United States Looms Large in Russian Elections,' http://russiaprofile.org/experts_panel/53857/print_edition/
7. Bureau of Verification, Compliance, and Implementation, US Department of State. http://www.state.gov/t/avc/rls/139901.htm
8. Tomislava Penkova, 'Russia and the US Reset after the New START,' *ISPI Analysis*, April 2010, http://www.ispionline.it/it/documents/Analysis_7_2010.pdf, p.5.
9. Robert Levgold, 'Papporteur's Summary: US-Russia Relations: Policy Challenges for the Congress,' Vol. 25, no.1, 15–21 February 2010, The Aspen Institute, Washington DC, p. 3.
10. 'Ratify the New Start Treaty,' *The New York Times* Editorial, 14 September 2010, http://www.nytimes.com/2010/09/15/opinion/15wed1.html
11. The Library of Congress, Treaties 111th Congress, Treaty Number 111-5, http://thomas.loc.gov/cgi-bin/ntquery/z?trtys:111TD00005
12. Investments in Conventional Prompt Global Strike, Bureau of Arms Control, Verification and Compliance, US Department of State, http://www.state.gov/t/avc/rls/152730.htm
13. Remarks By the President on Strengthening Missile Defence In Europe, The White House, 17 September 2009, http://www.whitehouse.gov/the-press-office/remarks-president-strengthening-missile- defence -europe
14. 'New Missile Shield in Romania Tests Russian-US Relations,' *Xinhua*, 5 May 2011, http://www.chinadaily.com.cn/xinhua/2011-05-05/content_2517259.html
15. The US Ambassador to Russia, who at that time was NSC Director for Russian and Eurasian Affairs.

16. Christi Parsons, 'For Obama and Medvedev, some Cold War-style Frost over Missile Defence,' *The Los Angeles Times*, 27 May 2011. http://articles.latimes.com/2011/may/27/news/la-pn-obama-medvedev-missile-defence-20110527
17. 'Red Button or Reset Button?' *The Washington Times* Editorial, 1 June 2011, http://www.washingtontimes.com/news/2011/jun/1/red-button-or-reset-button/
18. Simon Shuster, 'Russia Wants a Finger on Europe's Nuclear Shield,' *TIME*, 24 May 2011, http://www.time.com/time/world/article/0,8599,2073757,00.html
19. 'Missile Defense Cooperation Could Change Game,' http://www.aviationweek.com/aw/generic/story_channel.jsp?channel=defence &id=news/awx/2012/02/06/awx_02_06_2012_p0-421552.xml&headline=Missile%20 defence %20Cooperation%20Could%20Change%20Game
20. Roland Oliphant, 'Obama May Push for Jackson-Vanik Repeal,' *The Moscow Times*, 26 January 2012, http://www.themoscowtimes.com/mobile/article/451707.html
21. Remarks by the President in State of the Union Address, 24 January 2012, http://www.whitehouse.gov/the-press-office/2012/01/24/remarks-president-state-union-address
22. William McQuillen, 'Cold-War Law Blocks Doubling US Trade With Russia Under WTO,' 13 December 2011, http://www.bloomberg.com/news/2011-12-13/-74-law-blocks-doubling-u-s-trade-with-russia.html
23. 'US, Russia Reach Trade Terms,' *The Daily Beast*, 12 October 2011, http://www.thedailybeast.com/articles/2011/10/12/u-s-russian-trade-negotiators-solve-key-issues-blocking-moscow-s-wto-entry.html
24. 'US, Russia Reach Trade Terms,' *The Daily Beast*, 12 October 2011, http://www.thedailybeast.com/articles/2011/10/12/u-s-russian-trade-negotiators-solve-key-issues-blocking-moscow-s-wto-entry.html
25. Rachel S. Salzman, *US Policy Toward Russia: A Review of Policy*

Recommendations, Carnegie Corporation of New York, May 2010, p. 50.

26. Interview given by Dmitry Medvedev to Television Channel Channel One, Rossia, NTV, Official Website of the President of Russia, http://archive.kremlin.ru/eng/speeches/2008/08/31/1850_type82912type82916_206003.shtml
27. Dmitry Trenin, 'Russia's Spheres of Interest, not Influence,' *The Washington Quarterly*, October 2009, p. 9.
28. Salzman, op cit p. 48.
29. Trenin, op cit p.1.
30. Taisuke Abiru, *Iran and the Resetting of US-Russia Relations*, The Tokyo Foundation, http://www.tokyofoundation.org/en/topics/eurasia-information-network/resetting-us-russia-relations
31. Yanukovych says 'no' to Missile Defence, *UPI News*, http://www.upi.com/Top_News/Special/2011/06/23/Yanukovych-says-no-to-missile- defence /UPI-76031308824760/
32. Steven Pifer, 'Squaring US Policy Toward Russia with US Interests in the Larger Post-Soviet Space,' *US-Russia Relations: Policy Challenges for the Congress*, Vol. 25, no.1, 15–21 February 2010, The Aspen Institute, Washington DC, p. 33.
33. *The Right Direction for US Policy Toward Russia*, A Report from The Commission on US Policy toward Russia, Belfer Center for Science and International Affairs and The Nixon Center, Washington DC, March 2009, p.13.
34. *Ibid.*
35. Ambassador Rice's Remarks on Syria to UN Security Council, 4 February 2012, http://iipdigital.usembassy.gov/st/english/texttrans/2012/02/20120204154815su0.6453145.html#ixzz1llP7mZlz
36. *The US-Russia Relations after the Reset: Building a New Agenda. A View from Russia, Report by the Russian Participants of the Working Group on the Future of the Russian-US Relations*, Valdai Discussion Club, March 2011, p. 11.
37. Nord Stream is an offshore natural gas pipeline from Vyborg in

Russia to Greifswald in Germany. This 1222km long pipeline with a maximum discharge capacity of 55 billion cubic metres per year, will be the longest subsea pipeline in the world upon its completion

38. Details available at http://south-stream.info/?L=1
39. Details available at http://www.nabucco-pipeline.com/portal/page/portal/en
40. Dinakar Sethuraman, 'Exxon, Chevron "Land Grab" for Europe Shale Gas, JPMorgan Says,' *Bloomberg*, 11 February 2010, http://www.bloomberg.com/apps/news?pid=newsarchive&sid=aAK.6l3WmQyg#
41. Tony Halpin, Russia Stakes its Claim on North Pole in Underwater Search for Oil, *TIMES*, London, 28 July 2007, http://www.timesonline.co.uk/tol/news/world/europe/article2155477.ece
42. Angela Stent, *US-Russian Relations: The Energy Dimension in US-Russia Relations, Policy Challenges for the Congress*, Vol. 25, no.1, 15–21 February. 2010, The Aspen Institute, Washington DC, p. 26.
43. Andrew E. Kramer and Clifford Krauss, 'Russia Embraces Offshore Arctic Drilling,' *The New York Times*, 15 February 2011, http://www.nytimes.com/2011/02/16/business/global/16arctic.html
44. Guy Chazan and Gregory L. White, 'BP's Russian Partners Renew Legal Proceedings,' http://online.wsj.com/article/SB10001424053111904233404576458241367459356.html
45. www.americanprogress.org/issues/2010/04/.../russia_report_execsumm.pdf
46. Oxana Antonenko, 'Russia's Uncertain Succession,' *IISS Strategic Comments*, Vol. 13, Issue 07, September 2007, p. 2.
47. Eugene B. Rumer and Angela E. Stent, *Repairing US-Russian Relations: A Long Road Ahead*, Institute for National Strategic Studies, http://ceres.georgetown.edu/documents/Repairing%20US-Russian%20Relations.pdf

List of Abbreviations

A2AD: 'Antiaccess' or 'Area Denial'
ADC: Aide-de-camp
ADMM-Plus: ASEAN Defence Ministers Meeting – Plus
AFRICOM: United States Africa Command
ANZUS: Australia, New Zealand, United States Security Treaty
APEC: Asia-Pacific Economic Cooperation
AQAP: Al-Qaeda in the Arabian Peninsula
AQIM: Al-Qaeda in the Islamic Maghreb
ARF: ASEAN Regional Forum
ASEAN: Association of Southeast Asian Nations

BMD: Ballistic Missile Defence
BTC: Baku-Tibilisi-Ceyhan

CANWFZ: Central Asia Nuclear Weapon-Free Zone
CARAT: Cooperation Afloat Readiness and Training

CARs: Central Asian Republics
CENTCOM: Central Command
CIA: Central Intelligence Agency
CINCPAC: Commander-in-Chief, Pacific Command
CIS: Commonwealth of Independent States
CNOOC: China National Offshore Oil Company
CNPC: China National Petroleum Corporation
CPGS: Conventional Prompt Global Strike
CSTO: Collective Security Treaty Organization

CTR: Cooperative Threat Reduction

DOE: Department of Energy
DPJ: Democratic Party of Japan

EAPC: Euro-Atlantic Partnership Council
EAS: East Asian Summit
EEZ: Exclusive Economic Zone

FDI: Foreign Direct Investment
FMF: Foreign Military Financing
FTA: Free Trade Agreement

G-2: Group of two
G-8: Group of eight
GCC: Gulf Cooperation Council

HUT: Hizb ut-Tahrir

IAEA: International Atomic Energy Agency
ICWA: Indian Council of World Affairs

ICBM: Intercontinental Ballistic Missile
IISS: International Institute for Strategic Studies
IMU: Islamic Movement of Uzbekistan
IPP: Individual Partnership Programme
IPRs: Intellectual Property Rights
ISAF: International Security Assistance Force
ISI: Inter Services Intelligence

JNU: Jawaharlal Nehru Univeristy

K2: Karshi Khanabad

LDP: Liberal Democratic Party
LMI: Lower Mekong Initiative

MB: Muslim Brotherhood
MENA: Middle East and North African
MSC: US Military Sealift Command

NACC: North Atlantic Cooperation Council
NATO: North Atlantic Treaty Organization
NDN: Northern Distribution Network
NDPG: National Defence Programme Guidelines
NWFP: North-West Frontier Province

ODA: Official Development Assistance
OECD: Organisation for Economic Cooperation and Development
OIC: Organisation of the Islamic Conference
OPEC: Organisation of the Petroleum Exporting Countries

OSCE:	Organization for Security and Cooperation in Europe
PAKGLOC:	Pakistan Ground Lines of Communication
PARP:	Planning and Review Process
PfP:	Partnership for Peace
PLA:	People's Liberation Army
PNTR:	Permanent Normal Trade Relations
PSI:	Proliferation Security Initiative
S&ED:	Strategic and Economic Dialogue
SCO:	Shanghai Cooperation Organisation
SDPK:	Social Democratic Party of Kyrgyzstan
SINOPEC:	China Petroleum & Chemicals Corporation
SLBM:	Submarine-launched Ballistic Missile
SLOCs:	Sea lines of communication
START:	Strategic Arms Reduction Treaty
TAPI:	Turkmenistan-Afghanistan-Pakistan-India
TIFA:	Trade and Investment Framework Arrangement
TPP:	Trans-Pacific Partnership
UNCLOS:	UN Convention on the Law of the Sea
WTO:	World Trade Organization

Index